THE WALK

ELBERT "EJ" CRAWFORD

THE WALK

"He who reigns initially will not reign eventually.
He who does not reign initially will eventually,
Reign relentlessly."

Elbert Crawford

"All progress has a process."

ACKNOWLEDGEMENT

———— ᘔ꧁ᘔ꧂ ————

By the bounties of God am I able to thank and show my appreciation to those who divinely assisted me in the writing of this book. The generosity attached to this beautiful gift only verifies and validates the grace that our creator has attached to my life's journey. It is by the power invested in me through our beautiful King in heaven that enables my personal ability to give you the illustration of this text. So, first and foremost I thank God. It is because of you I was able to find my true self behind the ensnared walls of prison facilities.

To my amazing and beautiful mother, Andreia, it was your undying love and belief in me that fueled me in my battle with self. It would have been impossible to conquer the terrain of prosperity without the compassion and lessons you taught me as a child. I forever praise God for blessing me to be a derivative of a soul so pure and pretty. I love you Ma.

To my late father Elbert, it was through your leadership as a father that molded me into the God-fearing, family-oriented man I present myself as today. As you watch over me from heaven I will make continuous efforts to further the legacy of our name. Rest peacefully, Pops. I love and miss you.

Last but not least, I would like to give a big thanks to all of my unbelievers. It was through your expressed deprecations, verbalized opinions, slander, and doubts that made me understand and respect the process to progress. It was because of you all I was able to place myself under construction, enabling myself to walk a different direction, finding my center of self where I reached the ultimate destination…..my dwelling place of peace. It was there I rested and realized that the ordained struggles and hardships will be a person's best preceptor.

May love and prosperity be showered upon you all.

CONTENTS

———— ꙮꙮꙮ ————

PREFACE

———— ⁌⁍ ————

Life is a pilgrimage, a journey that will entail obstacles of severe difficulty and complexity. All laws of nature were created by our Creator to benefit every member of this beautiful human family. This book will lend itself as a guide for you, my beloved readers, as you embark on your life pilgrimage. It will prove itself to be conducive to the uplifting of spirit, unlocking the chains that bind our mind's evolution; the chains that confine the beauty and purity of every human heart. Understanding that the struggle will inevitably be heaped upon every human only sits on momentary platforms....a platform that eases in direct succession behind. The illuminated words of these pages will prove themselves to be dominant facts and definite truths. Once downloaded, these principles will empower and enable you to explore the terrain of life reflecting the radiant rays of righteousness and all that is attendant to its benefits.

The fashion in which humanity is created, is that of interdependence, therefore our primary intention as individuals is to flourish on our personal platforms complying with the supreme principles that our Almighty God established for our furtherance only to be walking examples for those who roam in the dark land of ignorance and blindness. By doing this, we enable all ways of God to be cemented in our ways, only ensuring the replanting of these exact seeds in the soil of other minds, constituting the enlightenment that is the primary priority for prosperity to spin on its axis, reverberating in teachings to our children, benefiting humanity forever.

CHAPTER 1

KNOWLEDGE BELONGS TO NO MAN

The key that perfectly fits into the ignition of productivity is coming into contact with the pure surface of understanding. The understanding that slothful perspectives and outlooks are the very reason why humans resist striving for the knowledge that if properly employed will give birth to the prosperous nature we all possess as humans. That pure surface will be felt when we face the confident statue of the seeker that lives in us all. Self-mastery will be accomplished when you activate within your desire to attain the purest understanding in life. The polarity that the planes of existence hold retain an abundance of significance and validity. The inferior nature of this polarity, however, only exists due to one's ignorance. This ignorance is the result of living and existing in a system that only profits and produces lucrative outcomes from one's blindness. The unwillingness in modern day society for humans to elevate, reach a higher wisdom, and force evil and wicked ways to vanish will only be destroyed when the unconscious person circumscribes inferior passions and keeps in bond their carnal desires. The arena of perfection is the dwelling place of God, and God alone. However, the clouds that darken our valley of faith is the mindset that "I will never be perfect." The foolish wish and hope, while the wise exercises effort and waits patiently. The highest heights of life will be reached if one concentrates one's forces in the direction of improvement. The force of one's power will become useful when it is directed in productivity's direction and counterproductive when wrongly employed. Little people have grown conscious of the beneficial outcomes when applying such knowledge to the world of the mind, which is the most powerful source of all. When one enlightens themselves, they have freed the chains that bound and confine the heart's ability. This is where true freedom is found. One must first strive to free themselves internally. In order for one to emerge from life victorious there is a war that must be waged; and that war is the lifelong war for self-mastery. As humans we are the most intellectual life forms on earth, which means we are the most superior. When this truth is comprehended one realizes that desiring the most supreme blessings is equivalent to us existing in correct form. As long as we remain ignorant of who we truly are, having neither control nor understanding one will only remain in extended bondage to knowledge, purity, and happiness. The external oppression we show on a daily basis is only a mere reflection of the frivolous 0.2 and fraudulent oppression manifesting itself within. The bondage that we place ourselves under is self-inflicted. Like the man who shows aggression and outward belligerence toward other members of this beautiful human family; he is indeed the artist of a piece whose paint masquerades the peace and tenderness that his canvas, being his spirit, truly holds. We as humans have always cried out for help, assistance, and justice through thousands of books, images, and concepts that have yet to deliver. We must give peace to ourselves. Following the inscribed commandments in our hearts, man and woman can direct all energy and forces towards the inward bondage that sits within our minds and hearts; and oppression shall no longer exist as dark clouds over earth or our personal existence. Once man yields to self-oppression, his fellow brothers and sisters will at last be set free.

Knowledge of Love

Love is peace, and peace requires education. With love being the greatest desire of every human heart, it is vital to understand why the barriers that hinder us from entering the arena of love exist. He who has possession of true love has embarked on his or her pilgrimage out of the dark path of anger. The struggle is ordained for all supreme beings. In order to reap the fruitful blessings from the universe you must undergo strenuous interactions with the inferior. Our largest adversary to experiencing all categories of love is the misunderstanding of the concept of loving oneself. It is our basic, ignorant, and unbalanced perspectives that truly hinders us from embracing and experiencing true love. Being that we all have the nature of being independent people, humans often disregard the fact that the nature of our beautiful universe is interdependent. Every living thing depends upon something else to evolve and elevate. Being ignorant of this draws the human further away from the land of love and closer to taking a front row seat at the circus of selfishness. Even with our submission and compliance to the worldly doctrines one will never flee from natural law. For example, take the young lady who is aware of her seductive attributes of physical beauty and charm. She makes demands on the relationships she forms and allows with a man.

Knowing she is the resilient element of human life she selects her mate solely upon his ability to meet these demands. Once they connect in physical harmony, conceiving a child, the young lady must put her childish ways aside and reroute her self-centered perspective toward the child. She realizes that she has to reevaluate her values. The self-centered mother never received the righteous education of truly loving herself; thus she doesn't comprehend the concept of giving to others. Therefore childbearing is seen as a hindrance until she allows herself to understand the virtue of sacrifice in the name of love, which is child bearing.

Another example could be the young boy who receives the massive blessing that love's divine land can offer: the bestowal of the girl willing to give one hundred percent of her love. Still the boy disregards the other half of life he has been blessed to have. Receiving such a delicate blessing requires patience and understanding. Such is not a priority of the self-centered young man. He takes advantage. Lies to, cheats on, and humiliates the young woman who is giving him the ability to completely possess her. He commits these acts solely for the approval from his peers and self-gratification of dealing with her in such a way gives him outside approval. Once the young boy arises from the young and immature platform of life, reaches the status of manhood, arriving at his destiny's checkpoint, he realizes something is missing from his existence to make it complete. For sure, his dealings with this woman proved itself to be historical evidence of what not to do. Solidified through his departure, deriving from her refusal to be treated in such ways. Upon his next encounter with a woman he has put boyish ways to the backburner and has destroyed his initial outlook on dealing with the woman. The man represents the strength aspects of life that have an abundance of force. But this battle, to ensure survival in life, one must have a weapon of resilience, which would be the woman. Coming into this knowledge man directs all energy to letting his other half know that in order for him to truly succeed her existence is needed. The young boy was truly unaware that a man's life displays only half of the ability to be blessed and prosperous; the woman must be present on the throne. He never received education on the other half of his ability to fight and win the war of life, which is the female, thus showing his selfishness hindered him initially from feeling the harmonious weight of true love that obligates his heart.

Knowledge of Route

In order for the correct routing of your outlook to initially take stride in the direction of harmony and beneficial outcomes, you must implement a system to ensure your peaceful arrival at the checkpoint of prosperity. This system would prevent disorder in any form, thus allowing the human to stay structured and directed towards their goal. A route is simply an incumbent direction, but as one takes this route you must be armored with impenetrable protection. This protection is truth. Truth allows you to embrace confidence. As you enter the realm of your reality the beautiful forces that govern humanity guide you poetically toward benefit. When one is disorderly, they waste entirely too much time and energy. There are many areas in which a disorderly person may succeed, although taking the righteous route would increase the success they attain by marvelous extents. In order for you to truly display the God-like aura of efficiency and speed you must route yourself on the expressway of blessings instead of taking the exit and truly hindering oneself by entering inferior communities. The nature of these counterproductive detours holds the most seductive and alluring qualities; being that the absent-minded owns the paintbrush that illustrates the canvas of today's society. The beauty behind consistent promotion of one's elevation and improvement by staying on this expressway is that where a community thrives somewhere lies a place where one can position themselves and have the clearest overview of the straightness of this expressway, as well as all other things that surround it. All of the appealing homes, businesses and functions operating around the outskirts of this expressway might be pleasing to the eye, even profitable or beneficial, but never as beneficial as the initial and familiar destination plans you originally made to get to. The attachments of these detours add even more difficulty to abstain from. This equates perfectly with life as a whole. When you come to this foreground of understanding, there is where you begin a non-stop prosperity fixed journey. You then will form an acquaintance with supreme law. You will be sporting the fabrics of that law. Armored and protected by truth from all inferior elements you might come into contact with along the way. But like the man who enters the room of darkness and is unsure of his movements, one becomes unsure of their purpose when they encounter or experience interactions with principles they are not familiar with. Having knowledge of your route requires one to reach the particular knowing of many different elements, making up understandings complete whole. Being that the human's lower desire is often the strongest, one must properly prepare for the trials and tribulations, and comprehend the superior principles ensuring that the route is not disregarded or neglected. Nothing a person undergoes or experiences can compel upon him unsuccessful circumstances, for he is his own compeller. Just like the one who thrives off of the illusion of ignorance, existing as bystanders and watchers, as you execute your plan on your route, reaching your checkpoint, it is by their own free will that they reside in the dark cluttered communities of unconsciousness. Allowing these disrupted and disturbed residents to draw you away from your route will cause you to exist on a totally different plane, and in a totally different form. Your new foundation of being will have been artificially assumed. By the illusionary elements of ignorance and evil forcing you to take a different direction, your most genuine nature of self would have been abolished of purity and supremacy. With these beautiful articles of beings suspended from intention, one will take inferior exits leaving the promising destination abandoned; thus allowing the focused one to assume position on their least desired platform. By entering into inferior standings, one experiences arrested development, changing back to the barbaric behaviors and outlaws that were once abandoned.

Once the route to success has been altered you have to re-evaluate the steps you have taken. Starting at the initial take off spot will ensure you are properly prepared to trample over the adversity that has been created. This unexpected adversity will prove itself to be problematic if your armor of truth is able to be penetrated. The most common hindrance of the re-routings we undergo is that while positioning our armor, elements of the same illusionary and frivolous opponent that has already won previous battles still linger.

The plate armor of life, that guards the heart, is the internal confirmation of protection from our creator as we fight with the dark nature of all inferior things. The helmet is the guard of knowledge. As this journey is set out upon it is vital to understand that certain times, circumstances, and situations do not permit one to speak out what they know or feel. Obstacles are a part of the journey of prosperity, but in order to stay on track and never deviate from one's route it is a powerful tool to understand that a lot of our battles are created by our own volition. The expanded intellectual capacity one has acquired through extensive studying must be bestowed at specific and fruitful times.

The breastplate is the shield of all the temptation that will approach you while striving for the purification of one's inner self. These and many other parts of the plate armor of life will protect and serve also as a reminder to stay truthful despite the infectious environments one may find themselves in. The person whose foundation of living in honesty may fail momentarily, but his failure will define itself solely by honor. Your failures are the very result of striving in a particular direction. This will only serve as a means to lead you in the direction the most high paved especially for you, permitting the full embracing of success.

Knowledge of Time

It has been said that on average we will sleep for twenty-six years; so, having knowledge of time is very important to the person who is striving to cement success in their lives. Every hour of every day should be dedicated to something productive and beneficial. The concept of time must be taken into consideration for the sole purpose that it cannot be recycled or possessed. There is nothing that operates in the manner of proficiency that has not undergone the process of trial and error. Everything revolves around time frames. With this aspect of life holding as much relevance as it does, it is conducive to your production that you devote all time to reaching propriety's apex. Time seems insufficient when you sit still. Studies show that time passes quickly when we are absorbed in the engagement of interaction with someone or something; and passes slowly when we are thinking about how long it is taking for something to transpire.

It is your duty to leave a legacy behind, so utilize your time wisely.

As the man and woman, who is equivalent to total existence, embarks on fulfilling their purposes and duties, they must be mindful of the time frame.

To think of anything or anyone who is beneficial to the cause of humanity, or possesses a prosperous nature that does not occupy time and space or is immune to growth and development is an impossibility. Time is definitely consumed when you are setting out to do something, but if properly employed, time management skills will ensure one's completion of their duties and tasks. The remedy to staying in compliance with the importance of time and still fulfilling the obligations and preliminarily approved duties is to instill within the foundation of one's mind to never be stagnant. No object in motion moves at a constant velocity unless acted upon by a force. This law confirms that any object at rest stays at rest. The platform one positions themselves will be forceful. The only object that can act upon one's forward stride, forcing it to halt or pause, is oneself. Stopping for brief moments to strategize on how to overcome or circumvent momentary obstacles does not equate to a complete pause. This is the absolute truth due to the fact that constant motion exists when one is continuously striving in a certain direction and dies only when one forfeits efforts.

Knowledge of True Law

The complete backbone of life is chaos; shortly after law is established. The most abundant and powerful law is natural law, the law that dwells within. There is an order that lives within you that is truly cemented in your spirit and is not in debt to any external force. Nature is free and entails no restriction. The simple-minded person can only comply with natural law and truth with restricted understanding. Law is veracious, it brings only justice and equality amongst all living things. This divine order plays a very vital role in one's quest to reach the land of prosperity. The resident of this sublime order is the human spirit that sits inside your center of being. Outside of the physical being of oneself there are vast dimensions that are in no way held in custody by one's bodily mechanism. Everything in existence exists on the platforms of position and momentum. The law of momentum states that any moving object holds momentum, as one stays in motion, moving toward the checkpoint of life; the momentum and actual ability one is in possession of can only increase. As one rolls downhill, the speed only increases, enabling the pursuer to show the God-like aura of consistency, permitting the inevitable rise of strain and difficulty to arise. This is trampled by his increasing strength, granting him the ability to break through the walls of adversity. In a closed system, total momentum is always conserved, which is nature preventing you from losing or wasting the momentum that we all hold an abundance of. When one strives in counter-productive directions in incorrect fashions we tend to feel as if we have lost that momentum we were once so comfortable with. Truth is, we have simply stored the momentum we were utilizing on our journey in a place where we are unable to put it on the forefront of existence. We've become enamored by things that hold no true validity or weight with us, forcing one's superior state of mind to be infected.

When our natural internal order is infiltrated due to external forces, the natural position of supremacy we were once in is demoted to that of irrelevance. The thing about natural law is that its existence is concrete. One can never truly escape from this most genuine existence. Surely one can spend a lifetime of inferior standings; eventually, as time progresses, the supreme nature of the human will always surface.

Science is deemed actual; the scientific laws are beautiful and abundant. One of the most powerful laws ever implemented by our creator is the law of realization to make actual. For one to attain the heights of himself you must realize who you truly are. Our true existence is that we are nothing, simply parts of a beautiful order and plan. One's relevance only surfaces when you come into contact with these truths. You will never become anybody until you realize you are nobody, you must realize these facts in order to become a greater force in the universe. We are not in charge of when we die or why we exist. This is the responsibility of the initial nature that surrounds your life. The law of relativity is the backbone of the universe. The equation being $E=mc^2$ is the most accurate reflection of life. Energy is life. There is no force that exists, no activity we can be a part of; nor is it any interaction we can engage in if we do not exert energy in some form. Energy is the beginning and end of all things. All beautiful and righteous energy poured into relationships allows growth and productivity. Understanding this, you become aware that the surroundings of the energy from others, that you allow to enter your life, molds you into who you are, and this is usually done in the form of emotion. With energy being the father of life, there must be something that this can convert itself into, this is where mass comes into account. This world has many different meanings as energy converts itself into mass and the physical arena of existence starts to form an audience. As one is dealt with in certain manners the emotion, and behavior that is being directed, being energy will naturally force one to assume a form of response creating something greater.

What we have been taught and shown holds the most relevance and significance in the way we carry ourselves, appear to others, and engage into interaction. Energy being the father, our mass being the mother as they come into passionate contact with one another they give birth to acceleration. Nothing is possible of accomplishment unless one formulates a thought or idea; put that thought or idea into motion, thus accelerating from one point to the next. With this divine trinity working together, there is nothing that the devoted human cannot accomplish, nothing you cannot achieve and no height you cannot obtain.

Knowledge of Knowledge Itself

Your life is an everlasting war. In a time of war, one does not exercise useless speech deliverance; you carry out orders. The commanded order of war is to truly make the adversary submit to peace and peace only. Fighting with inferior intention or to fight for no cause at all is in direct violation of this beautiful aspect of life. In this society there will always be a war for knowledge. This truth is so relevant because with great knowledge comes great responsibility, and this responsibility is to always retain these pure seeds of knowledge and replant them in the soil of an ignorant man's mind. It is true that the masses have complied with the illusion that certain people are superior to others. Members of this beautiful human family have excluded other members from the table of knowledge, hindering them from consuming the scrumptious fruits of wisdom.

These tyrants of knowledge are not the only ones in opposition to the distribution of the truth. Unless one seeks to know and understand every fabric of being, one does not deserve to know that the secret of life is embedded within self. The one who travels and seeks is a moonlighted force in the universe because those who seek, of course, will eventually find. The one whose mind is destitute of truth is forced to forge versions of pure knowledge, thus allowing them to embrace and appreciate division amongst the human family. Creating a frivolous perspective that one is superior over others, which results in gossip, back-biting, and devious dealings directed toward the brother and sister of the ignorant one. Once ignorance becomes bliss it only spins on its axis, becoming universal; reverberating itself through the generations to come.

The ignorant are not always aware of their unknowing. When this is truth; the knowledgeable one must form specific insight in order to cure the disease of mental bondage that the person is displaying. For this to take place the knower must form an understanding in the direction of his or her fellow member. We only understand by passing through the gateway of experience.

As an enlightened human it is one's job to civilize the uncivilized and educate the uneducated. Being enlightened equates to the fact that at one point one experienced the blind life of being ignorant and lost. Badgering or harassing the one who lives in the dark, tantalizing them with the beauty of the light, will only result in one's extended flee from truth. You must teach with sympathy, not aggression, for aggression will only activate a deep sincere desire to retreat from the unworthy teacher. When possessing knowledge, and bestowing it upon the minds, hearts, and spirits of the family; you must have proper intelligence and sensitivity of the heart you are dealing with. You must be merged by compassion into whatever formation of being. You must comply with your obligated task; to teach, educate, and uplift.

Unknowledgeable people form opinions of others based on superficial and external assessments. Categorizing them by material evidence. There is an occupied space in the mental sphere of your mind. We inherently know what is correct and incorrect. The self-accusing spirit torments the person who complies with the inferior nature of existence. While forces concentrate toward the arena of inferior format, the feet serve as vehicles, transporting you to the gathering of the lost ones; the hands perform the duties validating this position. The tongue professes the action, allowing one to be verbally sworn to ignorance. Once these heinous acts are committed one allows the dark powers of the universe to enter, and the sole intention of these powers are to destroy and kill all hope. This will ensnare one in the web of misunderstanding.

Having the knowledge of life constitutes you to truly pave the pathways and roads in which the person will utilize toward his hard-fought journey.

The foundation of knowledge is basic and exists in the simplest of forms. The simplicity of this beautiful arena is that knowledge lies within your own spirit. Knowing yourself is true knowledge. To not know that is to not know at all.

CHAPTER 2

KEEPING IT REAL

————————⊃୧୨ᝌ————————

Oftentimes we adopt different creeds, concepts, and ideologies to live for and die behind. These different ways of life are formed differently, thus appearing different. Yet the internal eyes and perspectives of these ways of life point in the same direction; that's developing the righteous human. On the surface these ways of living lend a thought of opposition or one being an adversary to the next. However, in the original forms of these pure doctrines one finds righteousness in all members of this human family. Along the way our ability to develop was hindered. There has always been philosophical meaning followed by divine law when speaking of life's doctrines. Every human has an overwhelming desire to believe in something. However, when one injects inferior chemicals into superior substances the ability for that substance to remain at the apex of purity at that moment has been expelled from possibility. The key to life lies within one being able to develop in all areas, categories, and sectors of being and existing. Once one's ability to continuously develop is altered, the oppressor of purity can now socially engineer all ways of life; promoting division, which is the true work of the inferior minded. To be divided is to be sinful and wrong. Naturally we are adaptable creatures, we assume whatever form is necessary and conducive to our survival. By us never being able to elude the natural laws of love and harmony, one will reach the checkpoint of acknowledgement and will be scorned by the fires of regret. It takes misfortunes of great force to compel you to realize the divine within yourself. This will only open your eyes enabling you to see divine potential in all beings. When this takes place, you transcend past ordinary life to abundant things. These are not the true victims of arrested development. The one who has undergone devastation after devastation and remains on their pilgrimage of ignorance is the true victim of the world's vain game. But in all actuality, this is the human that holds the highest level of potential to shine the golden light of purity amongst the entire human family; being that the struggle is ordained for us all. The thing or person that holds an impenetrable surface sits upon a solid and cemented platform. The way "real" and authentic are categorized versus the actual meaning of these words are complete opposites. However, by bartering divine direction for error the original causes in which all different ways of life were built deviate from its true direction. When life loses direction, so do the beings who are a part of it. The originators kindled a light, and once this light was taken away, due to different types of oppression, they began to wander through the lands that earth provides blindly, desperately attempting to pick up the shattered pieces of the once flawless chandelier, blaming each other when one is cut by the jagged glass. Paralyzed by social gunshots one is confined to the stretcher of negativity, hate, bitterness, and envy toward other members of this beautiful human family. This makes us capital to a system that was implemented for that exact purpose. By definition this means our religions, our organizations, and all other things that bring humans together, were built on principles of protection, righteousness, and upliftment now exist in frivolous and fraudulent forms; being that the members and residents of these beautiful mansions of belonging are not abiding by or complying with its household rules.

In modern terminologies failure to comply with falsehood means that one is not "keeping it real." As humans we all have the potential to succeed and fail, to do good as well as evil. The essence of human life is often disregarded due to the system in which we live. This system only survives, thrives and improves due to the employing strategies that separates us all. Tribalism is beautiful and something that should be practiced by everyone. But what one must realize is that anything righteously practiced will eventually be adopted simply because that is our way of being. In order to find an oasis of relevance in the systematic desert we reside in, we need to understand that all groups have the same initial intention. True peace has no title, no category or definition.

In today's society, the biggest place of incarceration lies within defining a person. When we allow titles to stand the burden that is heaped upon us and the limitations that it sets, allows our value as individuals, to depreciate tremendously due to the fact that as men and women we wish to live up to titles that we are given, hindering us from fulfilling the plan the universe has already written in its agenda for our lives. Once division sets in, the victim as well as the aggressor who implemented this inferior thing, undergoes a process that will only bring about the proliferation of mental illness and unbalanced perspectives. As long as the egotistical nature is the foundation of dealings here on earth, and one strives not to relinquish this foolish thing, the shadows of pointless struggle, sorrow, and pain will interrupt the bright rays of joy, making days sluggish and slow. Knowledge, wisdom, and understanding must be the blocks upon which the foundation of your place of belonging is built. Being that there is no true beginning and ending, the articles and elements that make up those blocks, giving them a definite existence, must be just as real and pure as the solid foundation they are being utilized to build.

In this beautiful thing we call life, the words of pure substance in which we speak must be supported by attendant behavior. If not, through the perception of all listeners and by-standers, one will be put into the most fraudulent category, defining he or she as "fake". The most complex thing for a person to do is paint a fictitious illustration of themselves, the extent that one will have to go to equate the fake with what is real can only be perceived as absurd. Fraudulence will never encompass the radiant ray of truth. It will forever wander in the dark shadows of poverty. The smoke that one engulfs themselves in is simply tears that have been masqueraded as confidence. Those who dwell in this enslaved land refuse to tend to the cries for help coming from the dull attic of the mind. The most difficult thing for the abused to do is claim they are being abused, yet they take possession of their dark truths only to utilize it as an excuse to run further from it. Taking responsibility for being locked in this haunted and horrific place but fleeing from the explanation of what carried them there. The source that hinders the fraudulent person is misunderstanding.

This misunderstanding roots from one's education pertaining to circumstances and situations. The intention of the man or woman should be to prosper to the point of no return, to the point where truth and peace are truly achieved. "Proper education always creates elevation," simply meaning that without proper understanding of what you are viewing from the mountain tops of observations, one will perceive, speak, and act only with incorrect response. Every living thing on this evergreen earth continuously grows. The man who misunderstands life and its abundant blessing will only stand stagnant as the vibrational pulse of the planet increases. The evolution of consciousness accelerates at a faster pace, allowing the people who are awake to embrace the gifts of accurate acknowledgement. This gives birth to the peaceful and serene action which equates to the perfect function of the individual. Permitting the luminous rays of truth to moonlight the balcony of mentality, the insight of the pure ones will pave the pathways of truth entering into true life. Taking into account the perception that the deaf, dumb, and blind have of you will only present forged opportunities, heaping unsatisfactory conditions upon the complete existence of the momentary beneficiary. In today's society, in order for one to function without pretense, he or she must pay attention to every fabric and article of their surroundings. This must be done because the unbalanced thing of this world permits the enemy to ambush its victim through the smokey clouds of distraction. Once cornered, one's mental potential is taken for a pricey ransom, the victim of the world's vain game will attempt fraudulence, comprehending it as "real". This artificial atmosphere is created to counterproductively transform the sensitive nature of pure forms and functions here on earth. Being fraudulent is second nature to some due to immediate and complete submission to falsehood. The ease and contentment that comes with this level of consciousness is immeasurable because one has no true obligations as a man or woman. They have not even begun to commute to the checkpoint of transformation, allowing the mind to stay entrapped on the plantation of ignorance. The only way that this consciousness can be grasped is if one opens the heart and willingly allows the pure fluid of truth to be poured into the spirit. The heart of falsehood desires not the fluid of truth, the annoying and bothering pain that this antiseptic will initially cause one to flee. Cringing from discomfort and confusion, the human will see the beautiful healing process start to transpire.

The primary reason why most cannot function correctly or live in genuine form is solely based on the fact that they have not a sprinkle of understanding pertaining to what truth really is. They take the beautiful and harmonious bestowal of blessings and privileges, and convert them into evil, forcing stationary suffering. Staying planted in the soil of laziness and contentment, one will not accept the opportunity to stand still. Due to the fact that the poverty of one man is the profit of the next, he is left sinking in the quicksand of confusion and ignorance. True life becomes a foreign entity to this person, the food of knowledge is spit out and rejected by this person, depriving him of the mental and spiritual nutrients that one needs to hike up the mountain of opportunity. As dedication and discipline is implemented by others, applying strategy to advancement and elevation; laziness, hate and jealousy is adopted by the ignorant being, existing in a form that is not conducive to his or her upliftment, hindering others from the elevation needed to flourish and bloom as well. The interdependent nature of our universe enables all to be consciously aware, awarding the possibility for all uncivilized people to be civilized. Until we all grow conscious of the ardent truth, the same truth that allows particular people to rise up above all worldly things; the shadows of evil will never elude us. As humans we tend to go against what is purely correct due to the creation of the ego, permitting us without second thought to personally hinder ourselves from forward motion toward our blessings. Our disobedience to natural law and truth is exactly what produces counterproductive circumstances. The internal outlook to the external world is significantly vital and sensitive to the moral and mental upliftment of people. One must look past the earthly systems of today's world, being that they lend themselves not to any of the inner workings of the human. The inner reconstruction begins and ends with the inner offerings that one offers themselves. If one implants seeds of imitation into the soil of his mind, this will convert into action, and he or she is not truly being who they proclaim or appear to be. They lack control within themselves, but everything in this superficial and falsified world appears as if their foundation of being possesses true strength. This glass house of their success will soon be shattered by the rocks of circumstance, which will reveal the true identity of the fraudulent person, the identity that never truly belonged to them, forcing these people to exist as they truly are. Every being is born pure, it is up to the brothers and sisters of this human family to cultivate one another to set off the alarm in the hearts of the blind, waking up that pure person that lives within us all. The fraudulent human refuses true existence for a myriad of reasons, but a key element that plays a very significant and vital role in this falsehood is one's desire to survive.

One who shows integrity today will be chastised tomorrow. In the quarters of belonging in today's world, integrity is not accepted as a needed characteristic trait, so one who is paralyzed on the stretcher of life will gravitate towards the frivolous arena of existences, playing roles that naturally fits no true man or woman, a role that is only profitable to a people who exist on planes of inferior meaning. All of this is done, of course, out of desperation to survive the monstrous fight of life. By assuming this form, one is in a refuge that provides shelter from the raindrops of challenge. This is a challenge that one will be forced to face: the challenge that houses a force that holds the potential to break and disrupt the masses. By surrendering to those challenges, one only makes the war more hard fought, the grief and anxiety one feels internally will diminish harmonious energy, and promote a devious nature to be born and exhibited in its entirety. By refusing to obligate all inferior and frivolous elements, one is enabled to paint absurd illustrations of self, which only makes the heart harder and the spirit more difficult to be conquered by love. At the center of all fraud-like fabric of beings, there lies something so true, and so elevated; once awakened one will experience captivation that is merely unexplainable. Fraudulent and inferior characteristics spring from an internal battle that will externally take place if one does not practice peace. When the peace of the heart is disrupted by conflict and division it will manifest itself in the outside form of war. With the fight of self-hatred abolished this pointless quarrel of life cannot transpire and until the shelves of love are restocked with its pure product, the war will forever take place. The misconception we form is that we can end war by fighting against it. True love is true peace.

To fight in war is to fight peace; engaging in battle for the sake of peace equates to handing the prey to the predator. Once satisfied the inward suffering sits at an all-time high. This manifestation of outward war is presented and exhibited through the fraudulent dealings one engages in, and the unnatural forms one forces themselves into. These forms produce many roadblocks as we attempt unconsciously to enter the gates of love, permitting us to roam freely on the green grass of life. Embracing true success necessitates a strong moral foundation, it is commonly accepted to have an immoral foundation, simply because it is in direct compliance with the worldly and earthly systems that are heaped upon us. With these systems lending no assistance to the inner workings of the individual it allows one to be weak and to embrace the smoky atmosphere of true uncertainty. Even when the existence and behavior of the lost one is displayed and viewed as comfortable and smooth, he feels in the deepest part of his heart pain and discomfort. The one who roams in darkness always will possess a nature of curiosity and fear of coming into contact with something true. One is unsure of the outcome because they hold no dominion over the final circumstance which is caused by inferior motives existing in the form of his driving force. Being that the heart is the dwelling place of intention equates to all dealings and intention coming from the inside of the human. The person of pure dealings on earth is the governor over the city of righteousness that is stationed in the heart. He who is true is certainly bona fide.

Perspective

The proper view of life lies within the strength of the mental arena. In the world of one's mind it is a necessity that in order to view things correctly you must be at peace with war. The mental conscience alone is the spinal cord of the human spiritual body, which is the primary force that governs and decides your outcomes. The ray of your perspective cultivates the land of possibility in which you roam. By one's own volition will they avoid the potholes of despair and failure? The human will be as big as their most dominant aspiration, or as small as their most inferior desire. In order to truly ensure the completion of self, for us as an entire people to elevate ourselves, one must obtain knowledge of themselves. One must see that life truly belongs to the person that possesses breath. While in the grateful circumstances one should view life as a master tutor. Without selfish and self-centered thoughts one will start to see things as they are and not through the illusionary mediums of options and childishness. All counterproductive outcomes are only produced through the individual forming unbalanced viewpoints. These unbalanced viewpoints are due to irrelevant and momentary emotions being forged on the hearts and inflicted upon the mind. The systematic design oppresses the mental structure of others and infects the intentions of the victims who have suffered the world's vain game. The power of love and understanding outlooks is the bone that holds up the body for battle. Being engaged in battles and wars of life are the most abundant and important aspects of becoming who you are, and until the individual embraces the wins and losses of life with understanding and humility, the way that one sees the world will sit on platforms of incorrectness.

View of Self

All endeavors must reflect who the person is mentally, if not so, then the individual is forcing uncomfortable circumstances upon their personal being. Due to systematic design, we usually form inaccurate opinions of who we are based on the tangible evidence that reflects this exact imbalance. This evidence is based solely upon observing other victims of mental incarceration, who have significant relations and connections to us. This will display the corrupt nature of people who have been accepted by society and forced by teachings of things that have nothing at all to do with the elevation and upliftment of them as people.

As humans we form relationship bonds with all objects that surround us. Once the relationship bond is cemented by attachment it seems just as simple as it is necessary to have these things as elements that mold us into the people that we were meant to become. The incorrect forming of self begins to play its role when the hundreds, thousands, and millions of errors that are put on the forefront are exposed as we start to form and shape our own existence. Once this takes place, we have a keen desire to see the exact things and people that once made us feel as inferior as that everlasting obstacle of molestation. When we rid ourselves of this inferior complex and the damage that comes with it subsequently our arrogance deteriorates. The very illusion that blinds us is now lifted; the veil being torn, making unity accessible with all humans.

In conclusion, one creating themselves in today's world would be the modus operandi for unfortunate circumstances and hated past. History repeats itself only when the state of the mind and condition of the heart has not been revivified. The inferior attachments of prior circumstances and situations only stay relevant when the slave on the plantation of sorrow does not completely abolish his obligations to the slave master of failure. Momentary triumphs give us a sense of hope and identity. But the actual fact of life is that all ending outcomes, attended by unfortunate circumstances, are only a mere illusion created to forge doctrines complementing all adversity. Unknowingly these ideologies supporting the outcomes of the illusion we know as defeat permits us to embrace failure and accept success only if it arrives at our doorstep. The design of today's world is to keep the human of certain classes, backgrounds, and walks of life subservient to man-made procedures; keeping the value of fake things appreciated. Coming from darkness to light takes time and effort, allocated only in the direction of improvement from the person directing the energy. The substruction of the reformed person is the past, a narrative of prior events. As one navigates their ship and runs into all other steersman of life, he can only reflect on how beautiful the journey was by reflection itself; permitting the level of his mental and spiritual strength to continuously rise to the point of no return. Thus verifying, in his mental sphere, that failure is no such thing.

Accomplishment lies within the will of the individual, and in the will of the man lies the womb of the mind. In the womb of the mind lies life. What lies in life is whatsoever the individual pleases and desires it to be. By stigmatizing oneself, limitations are born, intellectual capacity meets a roadblock, and mental; as well as economic stratification becomes relevant, keeping all humans above and below one another; and allowing worldly and earthly systems to survive, thrive, and improve. As humans we are the matadors in the bull ring of life, controlling and holding complete government over the ignorant beast that charges us with ill intentions. The superior feeling of accomplishment sets in once our nature is exercised, which gives us a sense of self. The celebration of where we come from is only attainable when we acknowledge prior victories. Our past is us.

Crime

Law of man maintains a great amount of physical order, but the outlook that is possessed by the physical eye of the masses is unbalanced in various ways. Every individual that is externally successful does not have to be internally peaceful. It is not a prerequisite for self-mastery to be a public success. The oppressive and enslavement of the spirit that one gives up unknowingly to enter the dwelling place of physical progress is sometimes in direct violation of true law. When you put what is pure on hold to enter the impure vicinity of arrogance, at that very moment and exact location, one is forever convicted in the spiritual court of law. The beautiful thing about incarceration is that everybody on this green earth holds the potential to be neglected from this internal prison. Complying with this system one must make oneself stagnant to move, prove oneself to be insufficient to be sufficient, make oneself inferior to appear superior, which not only causes an imbalance with the human family, but also causes strife and hatred amongst people, which is by far the most heinous crime you can commit. You are absolute truth, and truth is the only force that can defeat and completely control falsehood. Being generous and giving is the attribute that can completely abrogate greed. You are gentle, and to be gentle is the only thing that can penetrate and hold the government over aggression. At the mountain top of life stands the person who is the best of providers for their family and providing for the beloved members who share life with you is the only remedy for the sickness of hunger. This is true law; this is true crime. The law-abiding citizen is the example to follow. The violator of self is the convict of mind, body, and soul. The person who is personally confined in self will never know the infinite and loving feeling of cherishing all living things. The introductory statement of life is identical to the statement according to which the universe operates. This preamble of existence is simplicity at its finest. Evolving in the direction of good and just purposes is the intention of life, but through worldly calamities and distractions, we sometimes veer from our path. These things come in the form of peers, television, music, and most importantly, circumstance. When forged failure is inflicted upon us due to the stagnant ways of systematic format and design we comply. All volition is then taken away from the will of the human, hindering him from complying with his righteous way. He eludes from the straight path that one's internal constitution of purity allows them to follow. After all of the wicked seeds are forced on the brain and unsatisfactory conditions are heaped on the human, at that moment he has the ability to let his light shine. The fundamental system of perfection that naturally and rightfully governs the individual is seen as irrelevant due to the physical and worldly failure one experiences from following the right way.

Acknowledgement

The only way to clear the skies of opportunity from the gloomy presence of adversity and failure is to concentrate our focus and perspective on the very reason it stands present; permitting the luminous rays of our spirit to shine over our lives and circumstances. Recognizing the power within enables us to defeat the Goliath of hate that confronts us on our pilgrimage of love. Being that productivity is our lifelong friend verifies the fact that unpleasant outcomes are our enemy. The sword in which we must use to fight for our nation is love itself. When we allow the unlimited supply of love that sits within our souls to take over, we defeat all enemies no matter the form they confront us in.

As Abraham Lincoln stated in a speech at the apex of the Civil War, "Do I not defeat my enemy when I make him my friend?" Allowing love to govern one's life enables actual life. The energy given from the human once he or she allows love to be their personal president defines life as a whole; being that life is only the exact energy unfolding in the direction of a righteous purpose.

CHAPTER 3

FEAR

PERHAPS THE MOST MISUNDERSTOOD EMOTION AND HUMAN FORCE THERE IS.

F ear will forever be a potential shackle, binding the evolution of human perspective. Believing that this unique asset to life does not play a righteous role in one's success and triumphs; wins all victories as well as failure and shortcomings might be the greatest ignorance of man. Fear is but a different weapon used to survive the atrocities of spiritual war. As one approaches situations that hold problematic natures, one will instantly feel worried and confused, which are prerequisites of fear. Being that one will only know things passing through the security gate of experiences, holding on the other side, the secrets and answers of life. Life's offering of propositions and problems increases the probability that we will sometimes be ignorant on how to utilize this sublime thing. This causes one to adopt perspectives to have fear. Once one expands their ability to perceive, you will be able to identify the goodness in fear as well as the downsides that are attached with this relevant and real feeling. The sensitivity in this understanding rests on the assurance fact that can amplify the potential for one to prosper, or demote one's position in the hierarchy of victory's chain. Escaping the wrong perspective one fears, one must view this force from holy heights. The heights that the divine resides in, the heights that the grand architect of the universe orchestrates from: the very reason why fear has such a beautiful bestowal of benefits.

Fear of Self

The one who is the possessor of their own personal existence, the distributor of their own deeds, and the pioneer of their own journey is truly the person who is frightened of themselves. As human beings we all hold in our minds and hearts a golden force, this infinite force is defined as ability. Every pathway in life awaits our conquest. Through the willpower and intellect that our creator granted us, we shall enter all gates as we so well please. As we experience and come into contact with the elements of these journeys, then will we learn that everything here on earth was put here for the individual man and woman to conquer together. That includes the treachery and sorrow we can possibly produce for ourselves if we are not very prudent in the way we employ our power. In order for one to exhibit and display this abundant ability one must flee from systematic negatives that are mentally and spiritually fed to us day in and day out. By allowing these truly inferior things to hinder us from self-evolvement you cast darkness upon your soul, chains that confine your heart, and ignorance that infects your mind. But these are the very things that allow you to flee from obligation and abandon responsibility. What man fears most; as a result of systematic design, is the true power he has. Living a life where human governments force you to circumscribe ability, the negative nature sets in.

Fear of Demotion

Everything that exists stands in the forms of position and momentum. When your position is personally solidified within your own rim of knowing your vision is crystal clear, you are definite of your future, and certain of your purpose. There is no obstacle in your mind nor any storm in your heart that causes a flinching step in your fluent stride. You are strong and confident with the engagement of interaction with people of the same qualities existing in the same place of knowing, this vibrant energy can only attract success. Your internal seed of desire to learn more will be fertilized by the external triumphs of worldly offerings. All of the results clinging to him, which are produced by his actions, please him all too well. As you awaken from your slumber each and every day your rays of intelligence will hold government over all prior darkness and doubt created by shortcomings and failures, those perceived setbacks existing in completely different forms, in different time frames.

When he or she is introduced to the true imposters of success and failure he sees the two in separate arenas and categories of meanings: making the polarity of his existence relevant, believing through books and adopting a perspective that is deriving from a mind that is not of his own. The worldly man truly believes that one, being successful offers only happiness, and that the other, being failure, offers disappointment. He doesn't understand that complying with these ignorant beliefs will cause blindness and anger. His vision becomes murky. His aura begins to become flimsy in its security and firmness. Exceeding all others, with only material and tangible evidence to present in the courts of true life, one begins to wonder why the worldly and modern definition of success no longer satisfies. The things that once drove them and caused the awakening of desire to strive for more is now depreciating in value. With only these things to hold on to, the luminous light of God becomes dim, and this is only due to one's ignorance of their purpose and position.

The first mistake that was made, deriving from this doctrine, is disregarding "your time." Momentum will shift and be heaped upon every member of this human family. But when one takes this beautiful blessing, that everyone experiences, and utilizes it for selfish reasons, motives benefiting self, he disregards those he truly loves. Looking over and past, instead of focused and direct, not taking momentum and utilizing the tools of this divine, God-given ability to benefit humanity, instead constantly breeding envy and jealousy. Because of the dominant truth that every flower loses its fragrance, it only verifies that these earthly achievements will eventually diminish and slowly fade away, leaving a man with nothing but his legacy of disaster left behind. If we start to use our momentum and power for the betterment of the whole, we will increase the power of humanity's wall. Resources and blessings come through people. But if pure intentions are not a fabric of the reason one is employing, that person will eventually be overlooked, without a second look being taken. The gloomy clouds of struggle will shadow that person's being. This is the ultimate fear of any human: to be left behind and disregarded.

CHAPTER 4

INDEPENDENCE AND SELF GOVERNMENT

I t is definite that throughout history all tribes, organizations, and any brotherhood or sisterhood have had their own independent oaths and creeds. When you make this solemn promise to the divine within yourself to be the confirmer of your devotion to a truthful statement or to validate that you are aware of the sacredness of the infinite promise you make, you simply swear to your heart to comply with the nature that every beautiful human has. Through these beautiful pieces of literature delivered in various different fashions, they all point to the sea of pure water that we can all wash away our impurities in. They point us to the tool shed where the hammer and chisel awaits us, enabling all humans to chip away at the imperfections that our creator gave us the faculty of intelligence to completely rid ourselves of. Cemented in mankind, the interaction amongst humans that our societal structure necessitates, we have a collective oath tattooed in humanity with personal mission statements deriving from one unified obligation. This universal consent of all humans comes from the creative force of the universe we all know as love. In the course of any event or interaction amongst humans, it is the job of the independently intellectual person to exercise their ability that attaches them to anything that is of superior and righteous outcomes. There have been many misconceptions pertaining to the word independent. Every living thing depends solely on other things to survive and thrive. Being independent will easily mislead the human, knowing the minds' sensitivity in evolution, the teaching of independence must be carefully disseminated. Being independent does not rest upon the basis of not having to depend on others. The nature of humanity's standing is professed by the protection of one mind to the other. Lensed through the strength of intellectual capacity and being able to lend all obtained knowledge to others, enabling the perspectives of the receiver to be expanded, increasing his or her ability to tread the waters of the ocean of life's tests. When one's spirit is tormented the soul is darkened with the clouds of struggle, your body deprived physically of the proper nourishment provided by means of food, does not carve an image of him that illustrates in any fashion, his inability to stand firm in his own rim of being. The strength and knowledge that a man contains pertaining to crafts that he has confessed to perfect, the same craft that requires one to complete difficult tasks day in and day out, can only be fulfilled by the guidance and teaching of others. The blissful blessings that are bestowed upon us by our divine creator will be awarded through others, making the natural seed of appreciation that sits within the soil of all new hearts undergo the process of fertilization. Through the sacred watering of life's seed of knowledge, this seed will germinate, presenting itself in the form of physical action produced through the response of this fantabulous gift by the person in the receptor's position. These are the very elements of interdependence; verifying that humanity depends amongst all positions held by all people to keep harmonious and prosperous dealings taking place in the land; allowing the family to grow strong and wise together.

What is the one independent responsibility of every human? The sensitivity within the understanding of truly being weak and dependent can easily permit perspectives and ways that trail these words. Is standing firm to what is righteous, permissive, and superior like principles true strength? This would in all senses amplify the possibilities of losing possession of all earthly things. Is the man who devours the soldier in front of him in battle, holding no regard or mercy for the adversary of his posterity, standing true to the principles that has been carved in his intention to survive, truly a monster? In the same sense, is the man who dies worriless in peace, causing no harm after life's shadows have worried him, life's lies has disabled him, and life's laughs mocked him; completely defeating him, willingly submitting due to beliefs, such as peace and love, which are not prerequisites for acceptance, weak and dumb?

The parent who broke his back for his family to produce earthly benefits but yet is still misunderstood due to lack of understanding and balance; a heart of purity but the rage of a bull, are they truly uncontrolled and heinous? This understanding lies in the breakdown.

Weakness

He who commits a crime ignorant to its prohibition should not be persecuted. She who evolves and shows resilience toward irrelevant points, cannot be faulted. The arena of weakness possesses many sections and sectors, but the basis of this infinite way lies in the person not having the ability to stand firm in position, having an inability to remain resistant toward the forceful pull of escape. Being able to vanish into the darkness of freelancing, not having to shoulder the moral obligations which require the human to exist as a true light in humanity's darkness. This is pleasing to self, but only defines one as weak being easily led down any path, existing as a puppet in the life of the truly less fortunate play. Once this light is shown and one continues to depart from this teaching, complying in secrecy with that of unworthiness, is one truly weak? Being covered in the muck of society's turmoil, one becomes an uncontrolled member of chaos instead of being the overseer of the strategy to abolish it.

Strength

Its masculine coat misleads many. On the outskirts of this pretty terrain lies hardness. Entering the arena of strength, one will initially be discouraged. The rough and rigid presentation will lead to advertisement that would cause anyone of any kind to possibly retreat. But as humans, we are creatures of constant and consistent evolution. That nature alone will encourage desire to see what rests at the center of this human necessity. As we prepare to travel through what seems to be a perilous and abusing journey, it unexpectedly softens, invites, and encourages submission to something higher. At this checkpoint of acknowledgement, one will see that strength requires you to protect what it is that is truly vulnerable in your heart. Guarding it with desperation and all of its attachments. All too true, strength is also the ability to acknowledge, with the utmost logic and sincerity, without favoring the blows that life has on the human mind and spirit. Where a person personally stands, they have simply entered into the kingdom of their own heart. The people and things that he or she depends or leans on are identical reflections of that person themselves; we are they and they are we. For example, a woman who exists for the sole purpose of completing her husband's rim of existence stands next to him; that is, by the power and allowance of God, one complete force. A single standing is too weak of a presence for the greatness of perfection. By allowing the complete terrain of life to be covered by one's resources, which will primarily become accessible to other humans. This is while still maintaining loyalty and honor to all obligations and responsibilities, the assumed form equates to nothing less than perfection and beauty. With family being the unflinching step in any communities' stride, and with marriage being the bricks with stabilize the residence of the illuminated ones, protecting them from all inferior and unworthy contact, the interdependent nature of the entire world is verified to be one interdependent force, which fights off the sorrows, pains, and the uncomfortability of life's underworld.

The Other Side

Many doctrines reflect from worldly perspectives, that standing physically, mentally, spiritually, and emotionally alone in every arena of existence is the only way. This imbalance in understanding we have as receptors, is due to the truth that the world's infection lies in the spirit of many. Living in life where most are blinded by what appears to be pure reason and dominant truth, validating the supreme law, holding the weights of life on the balance scale of it all. Intentions are formed by conditions of self. If the majority's condition of personal truth is that they do not wish to be pure because of the pleasures of unobligated and easy lifestyles, evading true destiny, obligation and purpose will, at last and of course crack the structure of humanity's mentality down the middle, making its standing fragile. Without true strength being gained, the wild-like side of every person eventually conquers the superior side, pushing the lower self to a momentary height of victory. Where the wild one resides is the exact land where ignorance, sickness, and death truly stations itself. Existing only as an animal, remembering darkening events, expecting and accepting unfortunate outcomes, not even conquering that battle within self, not even permitting one to stand tall against the excessive chains linked to one by an incorrect government. The blows of spiritual brawls, and the psychological oblivion that fears walls have us entrapped in, never allows the capable human to illuminate the divine kingdom with the radiant rays of truth itself. The soul of a human cries out for help and ceaselessly mourns to the man who views himself as an individual. As the epitome of the superior creation the struggle was preliminarily approved for every human. The sensitivity of this understanding lies in many forms. While we embrace the trials and tribulations that are predestined, placing us in dark and unknown spiritual and mental places proves itself to be conducive to the human. This is, in fact, definite, but the self-inflicted battles and trauma that we give ourselves goes against this universe. These self-inflicted wars are a necessity to the upliftment of the individual. These battles hold its relevance within the grounds of understanding that we are our own oppressors, and this will only be understood when one enters the arena of true acknowledgement. In order to begin the pilgrimage to the magnificent land of awakening the human being must depend on the elements that make up every situation one finds themselves in, directing them to either destruction or flourishing. The resources that must be utilized to rid oneself of burden, and the depending upon something that is simply greater than ourselves, which resides in locations that we will not find our individual person in. This mirror, the reflection, that independent forces are protected under the umbrella of many things; things that evolve from the unity of a complete family, not one person.

Self-Government (the correlation)

The human body must be by far the most astonishing and miraculous creation. Just think of the process that transpires in the making of this physical phenomenon. The fact that the beautiful creation of the human started as lifeless matter, transformed into a seed that fertilizes the ovum of the female, converted into clot of blood where it rests in the security of the womb for a set period of time; and from this divine process sprouts the form of human life in the arena of physical form. It is verified through explanation that the human body is made up of many complex elements, the mental, spiritual, emotional, and physical unfoldments depend surely upon these complex elements being controlled and regulated by the individual. How can human beings be the overseer of themselves without traditional and expected systematic intervention? This answer lies within the concrete truth that we all are born governors, this understanding lies in the breakdown.

Being Governors

When a human is brought forward into existence, it is granted many elements that make up the complete being of that individual. Seeing the world as a child is a perception of complete purity which is that of a young god. The child completely renders love in all of his or her endeavors. This is the government which holds dominion over life. As the baby grows the heinous game of the world roughens the edges of this sculpture molding for the future, being the child. The potential apex that all humans have the possibility to reach permits a right for all humans to reach that exact point. As this way of evolution takes place in this life; infecting or purifying; decreasing or increasing potentials to secure blessings forever. The government one holds over themselves is subject to change. Ability is an asset that all humans possess. Seeing the world for what it truly is will sometimes, and most often times, prove itself to be destructive to the ends of embracing true life. This will take place as one grows older, wiser, and more experienced, which logically permits the born governor to change or abolish the government that holds precedence over their complete existence.

CHAPTER 5

ISOLATION AND CONFINEMENT

———————— ༅ ༅ ༄ ————————

Introduction
The screams of the entrapped people

A s my pen comes into contact with the surface of this paper, you, my beloved readers, will see the emotional attachment to me and this chapter. I expose my heart's weakness, being a victim of the finest confinement. I also bring into light the desire that sits within myself to evade my own slave plantation. Human submission to any strategy or scheme that will result in his own imprisonment creates anger, sorrow, and frustration to be the relevant forces in his life. This causes the light that once illuminated his path to grow dull and dim, making him exempt from all prosperity. Being that family is the foundation laid to uphold the house of humanity, a man's loss to the vengeful opponent of the world not only subjects him to defeat but places his loved ones in a spirit of darkness, a mentality of doubt and fills the heart with many regrets. To the virtuous people in my life, my beautiful family. If my mental imprisonment, which only lends a personal walkway to me for my physical and spiritual incarceration, ever made you doubtful that I would ever assume the form of a real man, leader, and provide for you; if I ever made you regretful of my placement in your journey and this led to your departure from me in this life because I failed to exist as you needed me to, I truly understand. A voice in my heart cries out in apology, and from the depths of my heart I ask for your forgiveness. I love you.

Sincerely,
E.J.

The Beauty Behind the Madness

The foundation of reason behind things or people being separated from one another is protection. All external things necessitate the human to exert energy, concentrating forces in the direction of the distractions and pleasures of modern-day society. But like any physical being, once energy is completely dispersed, one becomes weak and drained. The corruption and impurities that lie at the world's center rest behind the misleading smile of the con artist. With the intention of taking every source of power available to the individual, the outside forces are the exact seeds which give birth to the distorted and ignorant person. The one with no understanding or respect for the beautiful struggle that the almighty one bestows upon all of us, the privilege of experiencing. Just like the physical makeup of the human, constantly and consistently draining oneself, will soon become unbearable for the person, forcing one to replenish themselves. This same law is permissible in the internal kingdom of man and woman. The sacred arena of the soul must always be restored back if the person wishes to uphold their strength, sanity, and relevance in this life. What lies in this sacred prison of the soul is silence, love, reason, and understanding. These are the ingredients which completely nourish one's life and cements success for one's future. Every tangible thing of this world is a complete replica of what takes place inside of the arena of the human mind. The initial thought of solitude or confinement lies in the fundamental structure that people are driven by worldly profit and earthly treasure they have been provided. The blockage in most people's understanding permits a standstill in one's journey of appreciation pertaining to the prison that lives in us all. Returning to this divine confinement for set periods of time, shutting out all worldly things, and reacquainting oneself with the silence and peace of that prison lends and offers the luxury for one to repossess the strength that you have been drained of, which serves as an incentive for long-lasting success. Once this sacred place serves its purpose, one will enter the dark and cruel world yet again, stronger than ever, leaving these pure elements under spiritual lock and key, where they will safely slumber until one feels the need to return to the center within. Unlocking the gates of self, locking themselves in to undergo self-construction and repair to fight life's everlasting war.

The Voice

As every human undergoes incarceration a voice will surface. The nature of this voice will resemble the initial struggle. But as this struggle is heaped upon the inmate of life beauty will yet again prevail. The raw truth of life will always overcome all. The governor of this tone is true joy, and the foundation of reason being joy is that every period of incarceration has a release date. In the idea of the tangible prison system a human's release date might be the happiest day of a person's life. The gates of privilege will open for that person, enabling him to fight with relentless power and ability. Allowing one to come in tune with their own interest and desires, permitting one to return to the innocent and loving refuge of internal existence. All the pain that people have caused allows one to approach those exact people with the willingness to accept the indirect assistance from those particular people in mending the shattered glass of the heart. This voice is superb, yet savage, an opportunist yet a significant risk. We can not acknowledge this voice as anything but God, and despite the fact that this voice is internal the spark that ignites the fiery desire to know this voice can only be coming from an external resource, being another human or the transpiring of a life changing circumstance. This allows you to become closer to God, the superior one: the only force that can free us from the gruesome prison of inferiority.

The Diary

The perspectives and opinions of people who are on the outside of your prison, being that it is built on whatever block that hinders you, will be that the prisoner (you) is that of scum. More than often, this is one's perception of self while incarcerated in the confines of that individual. Every person who is strong in one arena is weak in the next and will need assisting intervention in one's affairs to survive and succeed. This is where arguably the most precious and astonishing blessing given from God, is given to the prisoner, a diary.

This diary is not the tangible booklet we all know as a diary, but simply God's universal canvas in which we can express the intentions we have for release and prosperity. Shakespeare, with his famous quote of love: "Love is not love which alters when it alteration finds or bends with the remover to remove, oh no, it is an ever-fixed mark. " Your diary, being the universe in which you express everything that lies in your spirit, will reflect your love and joy. This diary also reflects the anger and frustration that lies in us all. Shakespeare's words make it obvious in a rational mind that love, being something that cannot bend, and God's blessing being a diary, will not resemble a small booklet; but a complete platform for you to create a new reality. Preparing you for the release from your confinement, our universe will always present itself in the open form of a tablet for you to write a lifetime of entries pertaining to life. Your struggles as well as your success, triumphs and failures will all be recorded here. Your diary (the universe) complies with your battle and assists you in fighting your fight. Enabling this confinement, we speak of to be a conducive asset to your evolution as a human.

Will The Tried Be True?

Time is indefinitely a human-made concept; created to measure humans' steps and acts to keep universal tabs on the fashion a person goes about in their life. The miraculous creation of time measurement does many things. The overwhelming desire of anyone acquainted with an adverse condition or circumstance is to have an assistant existing in the form of a human with a solid foundation present through their process of life's beatings: one who stands ten toes and two feet buried in earth's surface. Assuming the position of a personal assistant is the greatest ease that can be placed upon a person while undergoing a self-construction process. But the majority of those who are tested in love, honesty, and loyalty by the grand architect of our universe will break as a plastic spoon snaps under weak force. The most lethal weapon that can be resorted to in your battle for progress by the opposition is the fraudulent illustration painter: the person who intellectually sculpts the figure of love and devotion to you while undergoing life's imprisonment and truly not existing in that form. This will initially distort one while undergoing their improvement process. While one can never grow forgetful of the truth that even the heinous nature of all prisons is relevant and presents themselves to have extreme dangers and risk; prison is still a sacred place of protection. Protection for the prisoner because they will have time to reach the purest essence of self, existing as a true force, proving themselves to be a conducive asset to the evolvement and elevation of mankind; and yet all things are rewarded protection from the one in their solitude. This is relevant because needing confinement reflects instability, and an unstable mind can do all but assist humanity in improvement. But to no avail will the human upon release be able to shower the light of love and knowledge amongst the human family, if the same people one is revising themselves for are the exact individuals who have been leading them down a path to engulf them in misleading smoke. These are the elements that create the disregarding and animalistic person. The beauty in these people is that they remind us why we are so important to the human family even as solitude's victims. The place of solitude is sacred. It is where your light is found and where you are able to acquire the knowledge on how to let it illuminate the earth. Even the ignorant ones who know no true life and no true reason can see this. At what better time should one latch onto a light than the time while they are being tormented by darkness? Within all the battles that lie in mental solitude; being harassed by negative thoughts and counterproductive possibilities; this exact possibility of being misused and misled could all be a lie; being that all prisoners in some ways are mentally unbalanced; but only in one's own understanding will they be able to make the proper choice. This rests upon the basis of the universal elements of nature rendering you assistance instead of difficulty in moving forward truly being that interdependent force giving you individual ability to emerge from your prison door victorious.

Truths Pain

When human existence was created by our creator it was invented with love and purity. But homo sapiens; the epitome of God's creation, are creatures of evolution. When two are connected and forced to separate in any rim of being; be it emotionally, spiritually, mentally, or physically, a new element of adverse condition will surface. When the human is in a counterproductive solitude the smoke screen of the world is now powered and working. The two who are separated become prone to new ways. The detainee now sees life through its raw and pure perspective. This not only numbs one but makes one subjected to form distrust for all humans. Being enabled to observe all things in people, life's prisoners will now have the privilege of seeing the horrific side of the truth. Being exposed to all forms of knowledge and understanding one grows stronger and more enlightened about the illumination of solitudes' process, giving one final relief from the harshness that the dungeon of development will obligate them to face.

Is The Innocent Really Innocent

In the courts of life, before one is spiritually convicted and sentenced to confinement, the conventional criteria is that one is innocent until proven guilty. Most individuals are still in the stages of infancy pertaining to this understanding. Being that innocence is one being freed from the bondage of guilt: guilt being determined in the mind of the accuser. Is the person claiming the role of being ignorant and innocent to whatever charges are brought up against them truly casualties of life's war? The understanding lies in the breakdown.

Infancy is perhaps the most sensitive stage in the human being's development, being that one is exposed to the rawest reflection of self while being held in solitude. As a child looks to a father innocently for guidance, it is this very place that the sacred being must visit within self to obtain education on subjects one is ignorant to, expelling all possibilities of placing self on a battlefield where the complete format and reason of the war being fought is unknown. When the consciousness is expanded about the laws that govern self, realization activates. The human is now aware that certain circumstances and indulgences hold adverse conditions, being the opposite of auspicious results due to the lack of knowledge on how to fight this particular battle. If one does not know this divine truth however, and fights this particular battle in weakness and ignorance, violates law, and is brought before spiritual court, are they then deserving of confinement in life's solitude? Having to relinquish all ability to the locks and chains of life's resulting convictions, or should one simply be placed on the probation of existence, having obligated time to show improvement to the almighty? This answer lies in the heart of the warrior, which is you!

The Comfort Zone

What every person's intimidation and fear ultimately derives from that which the individual does not understand. The human's potential for supreme ability is what one is most afraid of; being that majority of confinements structure is implemented to force one into submission, to be controlled; and the only way the superior being on earth can be manually directed or held dominion over by another is if there is a systematic scheme to make one think less of themselves in spirit. The dark life is the easiest way to foster, one has no true responsibilities or obligations. The most comforting thing for the weaklings of life is certain confinement, being that they hold possession of the easy route. Once the gates of despair are opened, the shackles released, and opportunity granted to the ignorant, weak, and fearful person who has ultimately stopped fighting life's everlasting war will personally close themselves back into the dark protecting womb of solitude's walls where God-given obligations and responsibilities are eluded from.

The resistance shown here is a result of perhaps the most beautiful stage in life's prison sentence. That will be the day when the light of life presents itself as those exact gates are opened. Showing the wounded warrior of existence that they have the full ability to create a beautiful destiny.

CHAPTER 6

MARKET OF HOPE

———⌁ ᔐ ᔐ ⌁———

Who To Trust?

The hungry person that yearns desperately to fill the void of his stomach will accept any proposition proposed to him that would constitute his eventual feast. Whether it be at the expense of his emotional or psychological security means nothing, in most cases, in today's world. The nature of most environments presents foundations that rest on sacrilege, driving the moral structure of the people away from closeness to self. But at last, for the worldly human, and the impulsive ways of the person bring forth the tangible satisfaction and relief when the material that's desired is finally presented. The internal structure and existence of humans is the most sacred possession that we as people will truly own. When this is cast in the shadows of relevance the placid peace that one holds near and dear is quickly converted to chaos. The momentary pleasures of this world might in so many ways become more of a priority to the person who thrives off external things, giving one daily comfortability, who might you trust? Being sold dreams of prosperity might be the darkest market of spiritual commerce, permitting one to deviate from the tranquil silence of self and entering the arena of infectious and vain interactions which amongst humans is perhaps the gloomiest day on man's conquest to perfection. Breaking the barriers that block off access to this divine land must become top priority to humans, but first, one must train the heart and mind for the challenges that they come into contact with on this divine yet perilous journey. Reaching the banquet of life's privileged people only to reverse the market's aim and intention in today's society from that of darkness to the most illuminated arena of people's contact. Not to sell dreams that benefit only the liar but to distribute knowledge, guidance and love, even to the ignorant beast of life, reversing humanity's aim and to finally benefit all of God's children.

Prosperity's Hopeless Height

As the chambers of the under privileged life are open after being bolted under lock and key for extended periods of time, the easing comfort of eventual favor will be embraced. This is perhaps the most sublime time in the struggling human conquest for achievement. The lost truth that is usually cast into the oblivion of thought is that, as great triumphs await us, even more strenuous struggles position themselves shortly after. The fluent way of the world is ease, followed by pain. Identical reflections of this truth are the days being transformed into nights; days are luminous and prosperous periods, while nights are still and quiet times preparing us for the eventual trial that each day holds in balance with its beautiful ways. The fabricated truths that tantalize us day in and day out is that prosperity is an easy and peaceful achievement for the prosperous man. The people who present these ways are thespians in the play orchestrated to hoodwink its audience. Elevation was implemented by Almighty God, and made accessible to humans by the superior only to evolve the human strength, testing focus, relevance, and one's preparation only to solidify the balance of the universe we make up. By staying true to this aphorism one not only enjoys and embraces the fruits of advantage but is granted the ability to handle the bull of life's battles by the horns. Just as the prisoner who forms muscle in the chambers of solitude in mind and body not only experiences in fullness, life's bestowal of freedom, but also to assume the firmness foundation of standing. When, by the natural law of equality, the Goliath of struggle stands tall, eager to go to work with the warrior of privilege. The warrior who stands on the soil of the battlefield, willing to die protecting his sanity, only to amplify the possibility of embracing yet another prosperous form after the struggle is conquered. The battle is won and dominion over the life of the individual is yet again claimed.

Halftime – The Motivational Talk

Oh, blessed is the one who is able and privileged to feast with family. Knowledge is power and power deserves no price tag. The blossoming result deriving from devoted concentration permits momentary breathers. Willingness and support, only with the application of intelligence, is owed to all of our loved ones. As you, my beloved readers and friends evolve in life. As you reign as kings and rule as queens, remember that Almighty God exempts no human from his luminous rays of beauty and assistance, and neither should you. Hydrate another soul today with the replenishing words of motivation and support. Lend kindness to those who are down, firmness to those who are weak, and happiness to those who are sad. These ways are the ways of the knowledgeable ones, the ones who submit to the great force we all fear. The very reason that I know you are capable of this is because as I lend my compassion to you I am only half of what you hold an abundance of potential to be. You give me relevance, just as my mother gave me life, and as my family has blessed me with responsibility. The same relevance others give you only spins on an axis, returning to your residence of being's doorstep. Assuming a more obligated form of reason. Reason to evolve for the very people that gave you relevance and reason to shine your light brighter than ever. Giving thousands, even millions, the opportunity to love, see, achieve, and believe. Feeling the emotion of love, the emotion some of us have been deprived of for some time.

The Golden Fabric of Hope's Light

The beautiful and enamoring way of law gives the universe its very power. The law of attraction is arguably the biggest tattoo of circumstance. The almighty has a divine way of placing us in chambers of darkness for past wrongs, only to utilize our current sorrows and conditions to test others. The beauty that rests at the center of all this annoyance is that at the end of these battles, even the apathetic man will see the light of power and hope at the end of what seems to be the traveling tunnel of the dimmest life. As harsh realities sometimes destroy our dreams it seems that the way of the world is designed not only to drain us of having joy and privilege but to place us in positions of contentment of failure, sadness, and pain. As one roams the land of the lost it will at last become intolerable to remain connected to the tribe of the treacherous way. Once the human, earth's supreme being, utilizes adverse elements, not only to expand prosperity's possibility, but to increase the strength and humility we need to handle God's eventual favor; the courage, devotion, and the hope one possesses permits them to exist in his best version will reach its apex. This only permits the happiness that is housed in the den of the dark soul to relocate itself externally, showering this exact possibility for elevation on the mind and spirits of all of mankind.

The Fight

War is a propounded prescription to every member of this human family to remedy and cure the sickness of discomfort and disruption. The thing that oppresses us most is our deviation as people from striving from the perfection we all have the ability to attain. Operating as renegades, fighting for self-assurance. Battling at the drop of a hat instead of as warriors breaking down the barrier of life's most strenuous battles. The battles that lie in our own hearts as soldiers show a clearer, peaceful walkway for those who follow and depend on us. War with self permits victory on the world's surf. The polished and perfected warrior understands that fighting is an everlasting thing. Even the eye of the beholder might say that the warrior has failed to gain advantage due to physical results. However, the warrior of God truly understands that once the battle inside is won, and the soldier is one with their sword, nothing on earth can make him succumb to accepting defeat. This type of approach to all of life's permitted wars permits his hope to amplify and grow. This is the exact and identical hope that all humans' house. This fabric of hope lies within the cemented knowing that we are all warriors and fighters in a sense and until the majority of mankind looks internally to complete the structure of God's army, we will be incomplete because the warriors we need, not only does not believe, but allow the weak winds of adversity to shift firmness and willingness into submission completely abolishing the hope to ever be the governor over all worldly things.

Hope's Amplification in Forgiveness

As the clouds maneuver through the beautiful blueness of the sky with no care of capture or incarceration of any sort, they are always disrupted by the belligerence of storms and rainy days with lightning and violent thunder. Surely the supreme elements that make the presentation of placid pretty days and humans are at least annoyed with the necessity to hide behind nature's curtain while the darkness of its opposite often comes to the forefront. Just as this disturbance is now cemented, peace prevails yet again being that the peaceful and pretty days are a more desired thing in the eyes of the human beholder. The same overcoming must surface in the human as he or she is abused, neglected or misused. Forgiveness is the only remedy to the illness of hatred. As hurtful situations occur through human interaction one might portray through the delivery of speech that the mistake of others is understood and accepted; but lying in the soul is confusion, resentment, and reluctance about the one whom we dearly love and care about, resulting in abundant amounts of confidence lost in said person's truthfulness. Through the pure process of healing the antiseptic fluid of forgiveness immediately stings but later soothes the soul of the receptor; allowing the God-like nature in us to surface. Therefore, assisting our brothers, sisters and others halt in their wrongs. Bestowing upon ourselves the privilege to watch them evolve. Evading worldly opinion from the people we forgive, become stronger; not only for themselves but for us as well. Strengthening and validating the union forever between the two, which the foundation of hope gives us.

Hope's Adaptive Nature

The ability to acknowledge self lies in one having the ability to overcome obstacles. The human flourishes and evolves in any environment due to our complete makeup. The ability to adapt constitutes the ability to win. These obstacles and pitfalls challenge our will to persistently allow our hope and belief to rest in definite facts and dominant truths that are simple frames of mind. To have prescience about unseen things takes mental strength, some lack this strength. These exact roadblocks paint illustrations likened to a desert, a place of scarcity, no comfort, and unbearable conditions. These mental conditions forged by worldly circumstances spark the desire to conquer. Once this fire inside the spirit is ignited the application of concentration and relentless focus are employed empowering the mind to subtract our mental desert. Heat, dryness and humidity now creates oceans and valleys of possibility. Overflowing with the privileges and fruits of life, taking the infectious presentations of the world's inferior challenges and disinfecting its complete existence with the purity of success and prosperity. As these internal and external forms are assumed, empowering and enabling the human to strive in victorious vicinity. This experience allows the individual to exist with more strength in future endeavors he cannot yet see. Strengthening his hope being that this is what its exact definition rests upon.

Hope's Interdependent Beauty

Our courage to believe in the unseen future housed in the barracks of expected elevation is provoked and completely conceived through the deliverance of outside forces. The universal necessity of balance requires things to be imputed into the exact human who distributes hopeful energy into the surroundings of others. The cement that makes up the expressway of the individual enables their possession of strength to firmly hold up against being driven over by the villainous vehicles driven by bloodthirsty and cold-hearted people.

Their vehicle of transportation is fueled by the dark intentions of hurting and hindering the righteous one. This villainous road is exposed, paved, and rewarded to a completely different person. Appreciation to people is appreciation to God alone. A person's devotion to your prosperity must be respectfully likened to the work of the supreme one. The heavenly presentation of this person or those people seeing the Lord. Deviation from self-benefit is another submission to lending everlasting support to the supreme one which they love and care for. This support derives from the resting place where all life slumbers, the heart. When the heart is unable to properly function the existence of all the person falls into the arms of death. To keep your hope alive these people must be protected and cherished, cared for and loved. This location is the very checkpoint where your air, your breath, and your life begin and end.

Hope's Question

In this life, after all physical things are subtracted, lost, and abolished from personal possession, the only thing to hold near and dear to our hearts are the oaths and promises that others make to us; and accept before us. In this particular arena of life, hope's relevance is vital and important, but its evidence cannot be captured by human eyes. When the harsh beverage of life is tasted, within its bitterness, the reality is obtained that sometimes what we hope for is the very thing that will never truly be. As the brother claims devotion to the brother, the athlete to the sport, the man to the craft, the wife to the husband, or the king to his people. Herein lies the exact possibility that intentions are tainted, and dealings are dark and disloyal.

These very thoughts are sometimes the tsunamis that completely devour our condos of confidence built in regard to the things and people swearing these pure, honest, and righteous truths. These times of uncertainty exist and present themselves in sessions. Particularly at times when our confidence in these objects and people is at an all-time high.

When these dark thoughts are born, testing our strength to govern emotions and the potential for these sworn and obligated truths to actually be false and fictitious are heightened and increased; one question will always surface. This question challenges the hope we have within ourselves pertaining to these statues of life that we are so attached to. Is it worth it?

Within hope's rim the mental and spiritual illustrations we knowingly and unknowingly paint of these things and people possess the most beautiful standings within our own personal thoughts. The wings which enable us to soar over the terrain of the tainted people, witnessing the nefarious nature of darkened mentalities engage in interaction with one another, abusing, misusing and hurting one another consistently. This is the exact environment that we deeply hope the people we love, depend on, and care for are not located in.

The Hopeful and Hopeless One

Hope is hands down one of the most sensitive subjects in life's curriculum. When entering this course, the initial knowledge to be obtained lies in the category of the hopeless one. The beauty behind the chaos of darkness is that it must be passed out of one's life will it ever be revived. The revivification of existence constitutes the fabrics of blindness and ignorance to stand present at the crime scene of the enlightened one's past ways. Notice that what is good can only derive from what is bad, that what has a standing of favor and acknowledgement can only be a descendant of what was once disregarded and deprecated. This makes blissful one's prior hopefulness. Appreciation will only be directed to specific rims of understanding. This rim is the umbrella protecting us from the sorrowful raindrops produced by storms of evil and pain, the umbrella we once took advantage of and overlooked. These are aggregates making up the whole structure of the appreciative and hopeful one.

The hopeless one is now considered more than ever. As the sorrow of these people obligates the believers of change and elevation, new generations are born; all the while, the weak force of blindness is being transformed to comply with their jobs as the pillars of humanity enable mankind to stand firm. Brewing in the melting pot of the future are the new storms of anguish and troubles that our babies bring along with their upbringing, thus allowing the same heights of madness to resurface, after being gladly disrupted by the days of justice and hope, giving the hopeful responsibility to the hopeless.

The hopeful one is the one who detests that of contentment or acceptance. It is the people who impel the human family to do everything positive instead of destruction. These are the people of the true way. The artists of all portraits of peace, and the writers are responsible for the preamble to the Constitution of Light.

The Prudent Silence

Just as the turbulence of day would be demolished; with its attendant distractions by the peaceful and motionless presence of night, constitutes the true evolution of a nation. The public grounds of night are roamed and hunted on by the predators of life's offerings, pouncing on the innocent and helpless prey they spot. The hopeful and aspiring man's subjugation of self lies inside his household of these silent and opportune times. This is where the gathering of thoughts takes place. Cramming action into small time frames in moments of desperate measure is not, and never will be conducive to the success of a human. The conquering of a land lies possible at the heart of the blueprint which derives from thought and time. One entering their personal arsenal of thoughts allows them to utilize weapons to defend and protect every direction that the army of despair could possibly attack. One's true center lies in the silence of the household, ensnared within the physical walls of safety and comfortability, the mind is at ease, allowing the beauty in the plan to be presented through acquired concentration. This means that all fights are finished, and all struggles have been reversed in government, needing not to subjoin any additional metals from wars' battlefield; for they all have been won, accomplished, and declared ownership of. Where all of this is possible lies in preparation periods, where it is secluded and free of diversion capture.

When Hope is Lost

Sorrow and unwillingness are that of defeat, this is the way of those who have laid down. Attitudes, sarcastic, enthusiasm to the events of life stale, and their presence cloudy. These are those to avoid. The one who has lost all hope has surely lost all possibility. The possibility for achievement of any sort, the magnetic pull of these people only leads to the depths of the darkest holes, making vicinity a complete hassle to be in. Protect hope, for this is the ultimate source to enlightenment. The examples of the one who has led themselves astray from the paved path of heavenly results lies in those people alone. Examples are the only thing you can set. Application of logic is vital here because if not properly employed one's mind will completely transgress against this law, protracting efforts, resulting in excessive exertion draining one's energy, making self-efforts tiresome. These are the ones who complain about the trenches of life's land, not seeing the beauty in prescribed struggles, but only seeing the displeasure in momentary discomforts. One who is disadvantaged disables themselves, the human equates to a being that is essential to the evolution of earth. This fact alone constitutes superior results; the faculty of intelligence is then applied, and if exercised on the wrong formats of perspective one has personally clipped their wings, falling from the quarters of heaven to the slum of spiritual hell. When hope is lost, light is lost. When light is lost, life is lost, and when life is lost one is no more.

CHAPTER 7

HER

———— ᔆᕀᔆᕀ ————

Introduction

Traveling through the terrain of the unknown is the natural desire of a man. He is all too inquisitive about the necessity of his quest. His keen hunger to conquer is his ultimate motivational drive. From his physical ability his life is solidified in the rim of his own logic. What could the epitome of creation lack? This constitutes a laugh. Oh, how the egotistical aura of man can sometimes produce the most inaccuracy in perspective. As he travels his burdensome fatigue starts to wear down his strength and exhaust his mind. He is a soldier fit for the most brutal battle, so he continues progressing forward. That unknown thing which he is searching for has an energy and importance that even he can recognize from afar. Permeating through all physical separation he becomes weaker only in the spiritual understanding. It yearns fulfillment in quarters he knew not was even destitute of completion. As he begins to feel the anguish of separation between himself and that thing his mind grows weary, and his emotions become radical, at last fear arises. What possibly could a man lack possession of that would set him asunder from wholeness and sanity. Trench after trench he digs out of, branch after branch he removes from the blockage of his eyesight, at last he spots it. Bathing in life's golden pond his eye enamored, and his rim of being fully submitted. As man only submits to God he knows that which he observes is a dominant thread in the making up of the complete fabric of the almighty's law prepared to nurture all of his wounds. He is now balanced.

The feminine nature perfectly compliments his masculinity. This creature is supple and peaceful. Its obvious weakness permits his authority to become an obligation. The attachment is natural. The light permitted through conviction is mandated by our King who abides in heaven. Behold, it is her.

The Personalized Sculpture

The prettiest way of human conformity lies in the earth mother, woman. The totality of the beauty that lies in her resilience shall constitute and permit the weakening of any male heart. It is a natural tendency of this infinite creature to assume whatever form she must, in any given situation, to ensure her safety and comfortability. As she embarks on her journey of accomplishing life's goals the worldly thieves of innocence will misuse and take advantage of her precious self, forging unconscious movements, placing her into categories and stamping to her a file of existence, holding derogatory and disrespectful descriptions. Where she is not guided, she will be misled. Even through her perilous time, the pure asset of her heart is still a relevant and conducive aggregate in the bulk of mankind's journey. Even heinous and devious men are illuminated by the presence of her, whom he manipulates; ill his intentions may be, but her way is still that of light. The necessitated intervention of a righteous man into the affairs of a conscience or unconscious woman moonlights her divine attribute of resilience. ***God gives the man a gift of a soft and raw substance***. As the earth father exists in his natural form he molds and he sculps. Chipping away at the imperfections of his masterpiece to be he utilizes precision and patience staying in tune with his God like ability to create. He is diligent in this process after ceaselessly concentrating and relentlessly directing one's forces with this soft and willing material presented from heaven. Placing it in the heated chamber of life's oven, cementing the structure and foundation his intended energy allowed. The ending product is finally presented, and what you have is the greatest blessing to man that was ever given by God. His wife.

The Courageous Necessity of Her Masquerade

In the current format of societal structure, the division and disregardful ways that set asunder the human from compassion has most definitely reached its apex. With unity being a dominant characteristic of our universe, one will at last become useless to life's land if excessive engagement in worldly satisfactions are resorted to, forcing the creatures in need of man's compassion to lend a completely different illustration of self to mankind. This is the earth mother that is spoken of here, having to force herself to be cautious with her God given mate due to his mentality's confinement stationed on the platform of limit. Man's barbaric ways, which is only relevant due to the intervention of a system designed to keep certain humans stagnant, is the very reason the woman refuses to allow her luminous way to ease the hearts of all those whom she surrounds. Her expectation of the modern-day man is that of disrespect and complete refusal to build. As the clouds of a gloomy day make it impossible for the eyesight of the people to lend observance to the most powerful source of life's energy, the sun, equates to exact actions and behaviors that women present while engaging in interaction with other men. Allowing their impenetrable exterior to protect their soft and supple center, just as a crab would.

In order to unlock what binds a man's mind, conquer what torments his spirit, and purify what infects his heart, he must become one with the being that truly longs for him. The creature, who by nature, is connected to him. The one who truly fears that the opening of all gates leading to her soul will not be loved or appreciated, cherished or cared for, but will only enable him to dismantle and tear apart the very ability that the Almighty has bestowed upon her, which would be to lend life to all people.

The Promotion of Her Protection

The laws of nature were made as definite and dominant as they exist for man to utilize and manipulate to ensure his individual and personal benefit. This permission is the very effervescence we witness men illustrate every day, roaming all terrains and vicinities of the earth as if to say it is his personal dormitory. With this truth presented, it becomes obvious in the rational minds studying and dissecting this text that he is naturally inclined to stand for a certain cause in definiteness on the ground we call earth, the same ground we as humans have been given dominion over. It is logical to even the simplest minded human that when a human is granted complete government, whether by God given law, or by the infliction of man made systems, one must guard it with his life. Prepared and willing to relinquish the very breath he holds possession of in true standing of the cause in which he shields. It must always be tended to just as one cares for the garden that produces the ripe fruits and vegetables that replenish the bodies of the people that make up the family table. Without requesting much she requests plenty.

Her standing in the form of completeness offers life to all of man, but one must remember, the aggregates that make up the totality of her complete benefit lie and rest upon the basis of her body, spirit, mind, and heart being secure and safe.

The Sublime Center of Her Submission

It is in the human way to yield to something higher than self, whether one is a believer or not. The feminine presence of a woman amplifies the incumbent role of man to protect her, thus constituting his superior presence to compliment her delightful role. His power was personally invested by God to ensure her ability to nurture the young and elevate the minds of the children during the process of their upbringing. This is the blissful and still water of righteousness laying present in her supple way. Kowtowing to her masculine mate would permit the ordinary perspective that she is the only submissive being during the unfolding of relations between man and woman. Man has an obligation to serve humanity. In order to fulfill this obligation, as the sun plentifully pours its rays through the day's skies, he must be taught. The first person that a child undergoes tutelage from the earth angel we call mother, wife, sister, or woman. Men, who age exceed children and youth, are sometimes still in stages of infancy. These areas hinder them from fulfilling the roles and positions that are ordained by our divine God. Environments lacking guidance and order ignites the fire of want in a man to stand up and perform his tasks of being the protector of her heart. This action is made possible through knowledge; the knowledge that will be unearthed in later stages of life that was initially obtained from the soul of his mother. The woman's submission to man is an act of gratitude and thanks to him for accepting the universal voice coming from all women to men. Simply lending lessons on proper ways to love and protect, just as a mother delivers to a son. Her submission is only an identical reflection of the first submission to take place, which would be from the man to the compassionate cries of the woman.

Her Constituted Night of Restlessness

Fusing the individual soul of a man together with his feminine mate is all too much of the perfect balance, harmony and unity. As the day's gleaming rays of love's sunshine progresses and unfolds, there quickly approaches a particular night. The identical aggregates that make up this complete time is a desperate need, a need that man had made by his own control and volition. Willpower and the complete faculty of decision-making lies on the make up of the man. When he, by his own desire for righteous standing with God, he enters the illuminated clubhouse of the chosen people. He must enter completely balanced to receive the golden membership of everlasting access to heaven. The other half of his soul being our earth mother has a necessitated attendance to permit this possibility. The painless heaven God grants through the wife will soon be tested as night fall approaches on the prescribed night of struggle for God's pair. This night is a restless and sleepless night, a night that will cause questions to surface in the mental gardens of the flourished couple. It hurts and antagonizes us, but why? We must ask.

The devotion and obedience that is implemented to the father of humanity leaves confusion with the inexperienced ones. At last daylight breaks. This night was a night of separation, which is the way of the inferior life, and as unification and completion of the human soul is yet again experienced, permitting the sickness of separation to be cured through the remedy of connection. All questions are answered with the sublime, soft, and peaceful way of God alone. Removing the veil from the eye of the paired beholders, which they accept with loving humility. The God given gift of woman to man constitutes tests and trials. Opening gates of opportunity for this pair to prove themselves worthy of the abundant fruits that awaits their union. Once accepted, this time of momentary dissatisfaction can be accepted with smiles and control.

The Disappearance of Appearance (Just a Matter of Time)

When one comes into conscious contact with their God ordained mate the fluctuating rate of passion, love, joy, pain, anger, and questioning one's loyalty begins its up and down motion. At times we feel the emotions that allow us to do nothing other than embrace our lover. Refusing to release them to the battlefield of the world where they are subject to contacting the virus of misdirection and scandalous ways. The earth mother, being the woman, has a natural desire to conform to the situation that necessitates her man's contentment and sanity in this life. Being separated from this rock of a person we care for and cherish opens up a route where sorrow begins its pilgrimage in its attempt to enter our personal vicinity. The receiving of the woman is emotional, spiritual, and mental food. Neglect from man's desire to interact with this creature forces starvation, permitting both parties to endure the greatest pain. Tempers flare and fuses run short presenting time frames where this illuminated union becomes dull, dim, and annoying; or so it seems. The acceptance of these times as counter-productive is the exact constitution of your God-given light's annihilation. As priceless gems are formed during periods where massive pressure is present can be likened to the trial and tribulation ordained for the couple. If true love prevails, as it truly does, man never departs from his woman wherein making a failure of himself. All potential of him giving up what he has promised her, everlasting possession of is completely devoured for he will never embarrass her. His character stands strong in times of difficulty for he knows the momentary disappearance of love clothed in fashions of argument and opposition to her are simple illusions drawn by outside forces.

Her Luxurious Call

As underestimated as she is at times it is overly definite that the woman is quite the sculptor. Through the queen the king is granted, from the almighty God we all fear and serve, the route pushing his journey across the complete terrain of life. Having the knowledge and devotion to create for himself water, existing as purity and compassion for others to hydrate himself, for he will become fatigued as the exertion of energy drains him in his attempt to shed light on the dark and ignorant people. When a man exists on this mental plantation, where resources are scarce and ability is limited due to the entrapment of the mind, he has lost the consciousness of the prettiest blessing of all granted to the human; the ability given through our make up to fully acquaint thought, a sound, and speak words. When we speak to our creator in the form of prayer or listen to his answers in the form of meditation, it is all expressed in a similar fashion as a voice.

Harmonious calls made to God can only be likened to the most beautiful sound on this planet, the giving to man in the form of vocal deliverance deriving from the throat of his most abundant blessing of perfection. Existing in the form of the woman can only be the second. Outside of prayer there is not a more soothing sound than the voice of the mother of civilization. Allow her voice to cultivate you, molding all people into the prettiest, loving, and most attractive forms. Presented as the most promising service to heaven in the most attractive forms. Presented as the most attractive product for God to utilize as we stand at his gates on judgment day.

One Thousand Watts

The electrifying feeling that she gives is all too much of a beautiful condition. This condition is not easily achieved with all worldly things attacking her, biting away at her mental confidence and spiritual stability. She sometimes will crumble at the brink of life's hardships, going through stages of complete breakdowns and defeats. The only way to reopen her alleyway of possibility for her to flourish will be by her mate having significant patience, speaking to her courageously and compassionately as her feeble presentation in hell's kitchen is presented. Her resilience permits her to stay in no condition except righteousness forever.

He must direct his energy and exert it only in the universal direction of evolution, and the heart of his intention must remain on the boundaries of love. As ships roam through the terrain of the beautiful seas, sometimes being shifted by aggressive waters, disrupting the peace of the expedition; so as she exists, sometimes being violently turned into the direction of destruction due to her willing makeup. Man's purpose, lying at the heart of his voyage, is to always protect and maintain.

When these forces are concentrated and these lines of means are resorted to she shines as the finest light bulb. Allowing and permitting him, her mate, to be the achiever and conqueror he was designed to be.

Pathway to Freedom

Startled she will be once the scars resulting from her king's battles are shown by universal presentation. Desperate will she be to hear compliance from him to her request to circumscribe his masculine endeavors. Any man that flees from the definite laws of life and departs from the vicinity where his destiny lies, existing on other planes, will darken his pattern of thought, giving birth to external circumstances that will disrupt his earth angel's peace.

The woman is God's channel, all satisfying experiences for man comes from his feminine mate, but sublime and abundant blessings reside in the soul of the one particular earth mother that God perfectly fashion for that one man from being held in bondage on the plantation of ignorance, darkness and evil; purifying perspectives leading him to the endeavors of the man who does good and forever lends thy assistance to the folds of humanity. Displaying unending devotion to her, the queen of the kingdom of upliftment and improvement. The other being a poetic blockage not allowing the voracious want to intervene and conquer multiple lands and terrains. To be the exact endeavor of endless agony, rebelliousness, and eventual destruction to her king. It is only she who can control the internal beast yearning to be released from the chambers of his heart. Her way is the strongest foundation of the home's makeup. His spirit of protection is what constitutes complete safety over the firm, yet fragile, standing of her. As she cuddles in the covers of his commitment she rests beautifully in the divine contentment of his way. Knowing that the covers that give her warmth is completely made by the vessel of his heart. She illuminates his confidence and supports his work, crafting alleyways leading straight to the kingdom of God. This is the path she paves.

The Fear She Fuels

Man, in the primary proximity of his own desires, is heedless of all things. All that he creates is delivered in a timely abundance, basking in what he feels is a necessitated pleasure. Surrounded by all worldly objects to prove his prosperity his eyes feast on its material evidence, satisfying what is only the uncontrolled animalistic appetite of an unobligated boy. At this point, the distance that sits between him and man's true responsibility is a thing that not even the most complex and sophisticated mathematical equation could accurately describe.

Darkness offers rest and sleep, but illumination presents work and duty. The spirit of man will become active and determined once the woman associates her physical figure with the eye of man, the forefront of his life converts from being dependent to being depended on. For the dark man, he has just encountered association with his virtuous purpose, and that is to provide. As the complete process of development must take place when the seed of what will eventually be a beautiful illustration of a flower is planted, so is the schoolboy who awakens from his slumber on a particular day. He embarks on his childish pilgrimage with his legion of boyish tasks to perform. Lays eyes on the schoolgirl roaming the asphalt of the playground with beautiful innocence. He steps, startled as all boys will be, orchestrates approaches and blueprints his presentation to her.

Consciously or unconsciously knowing that this girl, soon to be woman, was given as a gift from the construction shop of heaven, he becomes nervous and frightened. This emotion of what feels to be fear is the first stage of connecting two souls who had only a fraction of knowing, pertaining to their capabilities fully functioning as one together, this will give birth to the man and woman's ultimate appreciation for one another.

The Ants on the Concrete Pavement

Separation positions its stage of relevance in the direct middle of the God ordained pairs' connection simply because the masculine and feminine creatures, being the man and woman, will temporarily lose their way. This will present itself in increments that vary. Separation could remain potent for years, months, days, minutes or seconds, but never a lifetime.

The virtuous truth is that the soul that lies at the center of a woman's being, a soul that is an identical twin to only one man, will not survive without his completion, just as he cannot survive the atrocities of life's wars without her. Man's complete connection to a woman is directly akin to the word incorrectly used daily in this world where we live. "A man's best friend" can only be the counterpart to make his personal engine, of being, to run as smoothly and successfully as God ordained. A friend is a companion from which one intimately roams the terrain of embracing and interaction with. The only thing or person to fill this ocean of void is the other half of the spirit belonging to the creature that initially yearns for said completion to begin with. See her and love her for who she is. Just as ants follow the path of each other, in a similar fashion, man, and woman make their pilgrimage as one person down the asphalt path that God paved.

The Voice Of Comfort

A pyrrhic victory is for the man who relinquishes connection to his desire for women to grasp everlasting joy with his woman. Allowing animalistic cravings that once completely dominated his direction to be subdued, enabling man to experience the freedom that the express way of faithfulness promotes and provides. This commute that man, in his strongest state, decides to make after demolishing all boyish ways will feel the emotion of true happiness, gaining control of his life's rim. Most men, in their most vulnerable state of faithfulness, necessitate reassurance coming from the speech and behavior of his woman. The two most beautiful sounds that have ever greeted the human ear are harmonious conversations with God and the vocal deliverance of a female. So, if man, utilizing his infinite knowledge fuses these two musical sounds together he just enables himself to access association with life itself. It is clearly quoted in scripture "Through her God's favor is gained. " As she submits with her simple words, the direction in which her words are en route illuminates her ray. Speaking to the creator from her soft voice box, her face glows, her emotion illustrates nature's canvas, for she requests from our Lord to amplify usage of nature's exact fruits, giving the family table security, joy, understanding, and love. Allowing her to call on thy Lord sheds light and favor on the man, for now our king in heaven smiles in knowing that his most delicate species has been granted opportunity by her protector, being man, to request privilege to the family. The same family that is descendants of her womb.

Flesh

The moist texture of her insides is perhaps God's most subliminal message, the physical pleasure deriving from sexual contact with her only satisfies the beastly desires of the lower man. Smiling in momentary satisfaction only reflects the issuer's ignorance. Being a male allows this alleyway of disregard to be accepted and tolerated in the mental sanctuary of the one who does not know. But the man, who is a creature of abundance absorbs the understanding that reaching the apex of pleasurable feeling, climaxing to the physical stage of euphoria and releasing is but the smallest aggregate that makes up this exact connection's relevance and reason. Its simplicity is, oh, so beautiful. The security that her womb provides is that of a human laying in the outside grass, appreciating nature's hair as the winds roam through its roots. Allowing freedom to be felt, security and safety will be experienced. The warmness of her center lends shelter to his spiritual and physical sensitivity in a world so dark and governed by hatred's freezing temperatures. As man cries out for her willingness to stay connected as he is physically inserted, one should never negate the fact that this form of union resembles the personal portrait that solidifies the truthfulness in the divine pairs' creation, which is indefinitely the illustration of the totality of our Almighty God. The moans and groans that are dispelled from the vocal cords, which truly derives from spiritual appreciation that one is now complete. The connection of the two provides the ability to do as God does, and that is to create and give life. Appreciating that is appreciating her. The breath that every human will breathe, given through birth for our mother's womb, is appreciated as the breath that life permits.

CHAPTER 8

HIM

————— ༀ —————

Introduction: A Call for the Warriors

The words here can be likened to the traditional chant made for the enforcers of life's law to assume formation. This assembly consists of men, the ones who protect the supple household. The law laid here is the blueprint for the God-fearing man to activate the God within himself. The marrow in the bone of man's principle lies in the fashion its format is made. To express depreciation for the internal desire to be its own governor makes it relevant that the man is but a male. Having only desire to win the race of existence to flaunt his stamina, painting superior illustrations over his devoted opponents. On the contrary, you have on display the intention of the established man. Intending victory for himself only to reap the proceeds of this triumph to bestow privilege, favor, and comfortability upon the throne in which he strives for. This is the call to success, which can only be made in the form of submission to the almighty God who granted man to be the epitome of his creation. Adhere to your destiny my fellow providers, for this is the time of sensitivity and importance. This process for progress starts within a man's acknowledgement. Being able to pinpoint that you are the vicegerent here on earth is your first step to entering the life of blessedness and prosperity, for welcome to the land of the found ones, whose gates are always open to the lost.

His Naked Force

Man in his most gracious resemblance reflects that of leadership, strength, and protection. He is an enforcer of law and principles, and lying at the center of his internal oasis of self is the willingness to fight and die for his God-given cause. This is done effortlessly and requires no herculean concentration. But man in his rim of strength and ability cannot win this fight alone. Man often falls victim to the commonly and socially accepted ideology that he can truly format and lay his foundation of standing as a man solely by himself. Relinquishing and disconnecting himself with all subservient elements that make him able, he becomes fearful in his daily illustration. Being careful by movements and speech, only to convince all bystanders that he is truly the man he can only verbalize himself to be. He handicaps himself by complying with the believed mantra, "I can do it on my own". His ignorance hinders him in all endeavors and relationships, for he strips himself naked of all potential. As the homeless man freezes in the December night, he becomes reluctant to move, for he is protected no longer unless he acknowledges his misconceptions, observing the possible approach to perfect his imperfections. By utilizing all attendant assistance nature permits and exercises movements in the direction of evolution's vicinity. This is the only way, for if man flees from this definite truth and dominant fact his forceful ability will be stripped, for he is now helpless.

A Cold-Hearted Soldier

With two feet as the foundation of his body's structure, he stands on top of the concrete pavement covered in his blood, resulting from the excruciatingly painful blows that life will inflict on the initially unharmed spirit of man in his evolution process. The spirit of all men is, in the beginning of its existence, pure and illuminated. Because of lack of enlightenment and education, when the narcotic of lust, which will lead to intended desire that will never be, resulting in private pain, lies and fraudulence. This is followed by hope and belief in that thing or person, equating to frustration and hate.

Therefore, producing the outcome of one feeling worthless is internally injected into the soul of man, he becomes as dark as the surrounding elements of this world's proximity. Ready to deliver the pain he was once forced to feel, he becomes as numb naturally as these exact drugs of life make him feel. He is exhausted and empty due to his ignorance about the ending results of worldly pleasures and victories he expels and disposes of all desires to defend himself against the forces of evil. He re-paints his illustration of the presentation as a lost one. Unable to soothe the unbearable pain he has felt, he feels he is now feckless in loving others, which is the greatest desire of a man.

The Individual Standing of Himself

The arch nemesis of only man is that particular type of thing or person that hinders him from absorbing the pure fluid of ability to live out and fulfill one's destiny. People who exist in their most abnormal form that surround the ambitious man will do all but contribute to him. He is strong, he is the best of all others, yet others are the exact makeup of him. During the course of his life, in this rim of existence, placed in this modern-day platform, the majority of time he will be hurt, let down, and frustrated by the exact ones who give him his sense of self, which rest on the basis of him being able to bestow ways of escape from all worry amongst those he cares for. These exact conditions teach harsh lessons, forcing his hand to face harsh truths. When his standing's substance is adulterated by these things and people, he will acknowledge that he who is disappointed is only let down by that in which he depends on, and those in which he has faith in. The man who remains in his eternal kingdom is exempt from feeling the external outcome of inflicted disappointment. He stands firm, staying aloof from all dependence. Placing himself asunder from allowing the door that houses his faith to be open to nothing but the God that dwells within, and the one God alone whom we all shall trust. This is a pyrrhic victory, for what it cost him is a fraction of his emotion and a cornucopia of his interdependent sanity.

The Underdog

The personal rim of existence rightfully owned by every human being holds the significance of the most sacred temple. The element of ignorance that holds government over the blindness of man is directly associated with the largest aggregate that makes up the whole of potential, and that is simply not knowing. The illuminated ray of the conscious people is the proper light that lends balance to our universe. These are the men who fuel prosperous endeavors, lucrative journeys, and righteous outcomes by their ways that are illustrated through their walk and talk. The application of study and striving separates these men from the irresponsible males that annoy us all. The unmanaged and unconscious man however when tended to and motivated for change, growth and evolvement holds the same light as all other conscious men. Only with amplified force and momentum, being that the sense of power that will be felt when he emerges from the dark cave of the barbarian's residence into the sunny and fresh terrain of responsibility, will hold complete dominion over all things and people that once held dominion over him. The hunger he will have fused with his humility and appreciation one will have for themselves, as well as our creator who granted this possible, will possess the purity of the blind man who has just had his sight unexpectedly restored. To tap into aspects of self that you were once ignorant to as a man lends not only strength to your soul, ability to your performance, or even victory over opponents; but a story to teach to those who find themselves in the same battlefield you were just stationed in. The ability to circumvent these obstacles will come in the form of teachings, which is the most conducive seed to plant in the soil of humanity's mind.

All Aboard

The final call for boarding on the ship of destiny will be made amid receiving his boarding pass of purpose. Entering this arena, one is consciously aware and unbothered by devilish intervention. Their position is solidified in life's truth and relevance and is directly associated and akin to reason for acknowledgement. In this life abundance is given, but even after the hefty loaf of bread is feasted on by the worthy people, the crumbs also have a destination. This reflection is the role of the petty man who in his most genuine form was put here to hold near and dear his puny possessions. These are the penurious ones, the people who only enjoy the ships' sail, to feel the breeze of momentary luxury and favor. These are the individuals the abundant one gives charity to, in mercy of their tiny intention. The ship in which these passengers temporarily reside is luxurious, holding the work of the most gifted craftsmen and workmen. This beauty of a beast, being the ship, is the pretty and attractive channel through which God allows his blessing to flow through. These beautiful enablers exist in the form of people who bless the less fortunate, the middle man who conducts the transaction of life to the lost ones: the man who is truly happy in his personal heaven by just being in the midst of benefits bestowal. Through all of this ability and allowance the most memorable portrait is painted. This is the Mona Lisa of mental manifestation, but through all illustrations in the form of blessings most forget the most important part of this portrait. That would be the canvas on which it was painted.

This is resembled and reflected by the water that life's ship floats on. This is the source that enables all levels of men to receive blessings from others. These men are awarded the sufficient title, God's appointed soldiers. The water that enables these ships to commute is the divine pathway to God. These are the men that ceaselessly give of themselves. The men with no regard for return from any person, only from the source that constituted his being. These are the warriors of the waters, the waters by which life floats and travels on.

A Fearless Traveler

Life is a day by day, hour by hour, minute by minute process through which outcomes and results reflect its complete end. To live is to understand the value of the forward step; to make your pilgrimage through the alleyways of circumstance, to sail through the sea of condition, and to soar through the cloudy skies of possibility with no regard for external intervention or intending fear of failure.

Mans' ultimate purpose is to lead. Whatever fashions that may be to the massive area he covers. In his lifetime step obligates his fearlessness to meet, subdue, and completely defeat the evil that stands in the way of his successful outcome which presents itself as the ultimate prize for complying with purpose and destiny and submitting to the appointer and author of it. Love is the motive of man and the force that drives the universe. Know that love and grace is bestowed from our divine king in heaven. Dedication to one's destiny is the foundation of where his fierceness and fearlessness derives from.

The Center of Either

The universe in its totality is balanced. Negative and positive forces exist relevant on planes of equality. Man, in his molding is subject to entering one of two rims. Behind the closed doors of heaven's workshop men are sculpted, appointed, and destined for certain occupations. In every man's stage of self-acknowledgement, they cast mental coins in the wishing wells of form. Knowing throughout his process that he could have been created to either aid and assist fellow members of our sublime species. Existing as a conducive asset to the evolution of the human soul. Enlightening men to be protectors. Women to be nurturing and children to be obedient. Or to be of the worldly man, presenting only material evidence on the day of judgment. Living only for the barbaric pleasures of animalistic desires. Causing mayhem, chaos, and disruption amongst the earth's beautiful environment highlights his free will to choose. This is the heartbeat of man's want, to be able to acknowledge himself. Standing in the middle of illumination and darkness the clock ticks, winding down its years, months and days that are granted for man to strive to know himself before he is casted into the oblivion of the lost and wasted souls. On one hand, he is offered the initial discomfort which is followed by understanding and strength, or the way of the dark life, which in its beginning terms are pleasurable and pleasing. Only pushing you toward the ending result of disappointment and discomfort. In its entirety, this frightens man the most, for he who does not strive knows not the center of either possibility automatically selects him to be of the foolish.

Release Granted!

On this day, he is no longer held under lock and key in the restrictive housing of mind, body, and soul. He feels the wind that runs freely on the outskirts of his personal rim. He stands now as a globetrotter, in a state of supreme happiness; likened to the feeling heaven provides with appreciating his newfound access to the terrain of result allowing him to travel and commute with no boundaries.

His dark priors and past are no longer held over his head. He stands strong, for the burden that has just been lifted off his shoulders allows him to sigh in relief. Standing in the mirror of the ending results his strength is now viewed.

For those who, when he was confined in his dark solitude fled and departed after realizing that rewards from his battle are not immediate stand in awe, for he is now in sweet tune with his purpose and the elements of his mentality are pure and peaceful.

The Letter

Dear humanity,

As you embark on your pilgrimage in this life as an individual there will be a legion of obstacles, but there will also be a myriad of blessings attendant with your life's process. Always remember as the course of each day of your life begins and ends, experience and education will always be rendered to you. Know that the initial intention of creation is love. This was the intention of God when he created you personally. When the pathway of life that you are currently setting out on now or have previously set out upon, and the future directions in which we will walk, were paved, love was its purpose.

You must never forget that each individual on this earth operates, moves, and deals out of complete love or the desire for a particular result. The need or want for specific outcomes are the driving force of every human. Whether they have evil ways and teachings given to them or whether their heart was handled by gentle hands plays a role in this truth. Being a student of life is the most beneficial position one can put themselves in. Anger is a demon that torments the good. Take all experiences and results as a teaching directly from the front of life's classroom.

Trust and believe that God is our leader and governor will be the only asset you need to ensure prosperity and happiness.

The ultimate goal of this book is to expose my spirit to you, rendering lessons given by our King in Heaven to assist you in your personal lives. The foundation of these writings is to inform you of one thing: righteousness conquers all.

God bless you.

About the Author

—————⟫⟨⟫⟨—————

ELBERT CRAWFORD IV is a Little Rock, Arkansas native who's overcome many obstacles in his young adult life. He pushes positivity and growth for inner city communities and kids. While serving a seven-year prison term, EJ decided to express the process of enlightenment to the world. In prison, he sat and produced "The Walk," an in-depth layout of how we humans and individuals can reach a checkpoint of power and illumination that not a soul can take from us!